CHRISTIAN BASICS

A Tool to Grow A Vibrant Christian Faith

JAMES F. REED

Copyright © 2014 by James F. Reed

Christian Basics
A Tool to Grow A Vibrant Christian Faith
by James F. Reed

Printed in the United States of America

ISBN 9781498402651

Edited by Xulon Press

Scripture quotations taken from the New International Version (NIV). Copyright © 1973, 1978, 1984, 2011 by Biblica, Inc.™. Used by permission. All rights reserved.

www.xulonpress.com

I will be forever grateful and humbled by the many people who have helped in the editing process of this book. I could not have done this without their help and encouragement.

I am humbly grateful for all the people who have financially supported the ministry of **Christian Life Tools** over the years. This special help has enabled me to move forward in the Lord's calling on my life and has allowed the gospel to go out and bless many others as well.

A special blessing goes out to my wife, Brenda, without whom this book and my ministry in the gospel would not exist.

C *hristian Basics* is a tool designed to help believers grow in their Christian faith. After years of counseling, teaching, and leading study groups I felt the need for one comprehensive resource that would satisfy the need for the basic foundational truths of the historic Christian faith.

This book is a composite of what I have been using in my thirty years of pastoral work. I have seen many people benefit from these teachings. Also, I have presented this material with willing unbelievers and have had positive results.

Christian Basics is just one of the many tools featured in the ministry of **Christian Life Tools** that are designed to lead people to a vibrant and growing Christian faith.

My prayers are with you as you use this book to strengthen your faith. My prayer is also that you will find yourself helping someone else grow in their faith as well.

Blessings to you,
Ephesians 3:20

James Franklin Reed
Christian Life Tools
P.O. Box 2585
Spring Valley, CA 91979–2585
www.christianlifetools.org

TABLE OF CONTENTS

Each chapter features

- KEY POINTS outlined at the start

- TIME-OUTS designed for concentrated memory work

- ALERTS dealing with worldview issues and attitudes

- STUDY QUESTIONS at the end to help refocus the topics

- FAQ

Chapter One

THE TRUTH SHALL
SET YOU FREE

KEY POINTS

- The nature of truth
- The importance of truth
- The fact that faith and truth work together

" The truth shall set you free." How many times have we heard this phrase before? We've heard it from revolutionaries, politicians, religious cult leaders, and even impassioned movie stars. How can we argue with something that sounds so good, so right, and so true?

However, there is a problem with how the quote is used. The problem lies behind what kind of truth is being offered. Sometimes the most dangerous kind of truth is a half-truth. Can truth be so plastic and flexible that it can be twisted to conform to anyone's version of reality? Anyone can stand up and proclaim that their truth shall set us free. How can we trust them? Perhaps it might be a good idea to take a look at the context from which this popular quote came. After all, would it be wise to trust a version of truth if the very quote used to wedge its way into our trust is taken out of context?

THE QUOTE IN CONTEXT

Those who wish to sway others to their way of thinking often use "The truth shall set you free" as leverage. What most people do not know is that this quote actually comes from the Bible. More specifically, it came from the lips of Jesus Christ. To use this saying in a manner other than how Jesus himself originally intended can lead to trouble. Here is the quote in its proper context:

If you hold to my teaching, you are really my disciples. then you will know the truth, and the truth will set you free (John 8:31–32).

Notice the very *small* qualifier at the beginning of this quote that has some very *large* ramifications. The qualifier is the little word "if." It might be convenient to overlook this little qualifier. However, it might not be safe to pursue the results promised while leaving out the very reason the word was put there. "If" is followed by the word "then." Without the *if* there can be no promised *then*.

Some people say that the things they are telling us will set us free. They may not be telling the whole truth. Jesus said that knowing the truth would depend upon holding to HIS teaching. Only then can a person meet the qualification put forth in the words of Jesus. The freedom to which Jesus was referring is a freedom that can only be obtained by meeting the very qualification given by Jesus himself. If we ignore the very first word given to us by Jesus Christ (that pesky little word "if"), we may not find a positive outcome in our pursuit of truth. Furthermore, the freedom promised might not be so good either. We will come back to the importance of the context of this quote later. Let's briefly explore the definition of truth itself.

TRUTH DEFINED

How is truth defined? A simple answer is this: truth is that which is real. Truth is reality. A magician is skilled at twisting our perception so that we do not see that which is really true—it only appears to be true. This deception is all part of the fun. Yet, there are times when deception is not fun. To believe something that we thought to be true, only later to discover it to be false, can be very upsetting. Examples of this can be anything from a wrong medical diagnosis to a false guarantee on a wristwatch. We can all be fooled—and fooled often.

How do we determine what is real? The question of trust has a lot to do with determining reality. Who are we to believe if sometimes we cannot even trust our own perceptions? If a wild-looking man in tattered clothing with drool dripping off his chin were to leap at us with his claims of truth, we probably would not believe him. If a sophisticated gentleman in a white lab coat came out with his claims of truth, backed by a Harvard medical degree, we might tend to lean toward his view of reality. Trust matters in the quest for truth. Trust can add weight that can tip the scales toward the recognition of what is true.

APATHY ALERT

Many people have discovered that their lives could have been vastly different had they only known certain things sooner. People might say, "Don't bother me with all this. I just want to be left alone." The problem with this kind of thinking is that sooner or later the truth has a way of sneaking up and biting us. May God grant you faith as you take the time to read each of the following chapters in *Christian Basics*. The pages that follow are designed to lay a strong foundation for a vibrant and growing faith. This is an ALERT to challenge you to give your utmost care in your study of this material.

Before Jesus was crucified, he was brought before Pilate for questioning. Jesus said to Pilate, *"I came into this world to testify to the truth. Everyone on the side of truth listens to me."* A perplexed Pilate had only this sad retort: *"What is truth?"* (John 18:37–38). Pilate was face-to-face with "truth incarnate." He had Jesus Christ standing right in front of him. Pilate asked his question out of frustration and didn't wait for Jesus to answer. Unfortunately, he chose to turn his back on what would have been a rare opportunity for a direct answer from a most trustworthy source. We may not find ourselves staring into the face of truth like Pilate, but we should not turn away from the search to find the truth. Read and study these chapters slowly and carefully. Your effort will be rewarded.

Maybe you have heard atheists stating that "Science is what we know and philosophy is what we don't know." I would ask them if it was their philosophy that has told them what they know. They seem to have a lot of confidence in their own philosophy in determining truth. They have it on good faith that what they say happens to be true and is reflective of reality. Where do they get their faith to determine truth and reality? They have faith and trust in themselves. That is fine, so long as their trust is well placed and actually is an accurate picture of what is real and true.

TRUTH TESTED

There is a very basic test for truth claims. It is called the "The Two L Test"—Logical and Livable. We can apply this test to any idea or philosophy of life by asking two questions: is it logical, and is it livable? First, does the idea make sense? Second, can we live out the idea in the real world? Both of the tests of logical and livable can be applied to the truth that Jesus promised that we could know. In other words, we have it on good faith that we can trust that what Jesus has said is really true. We can also live out his truth in the real world. The truth that Jesus proclaimed should pass the "Two L Test."

The question of faith is of vital importance when we begin to sort out what is true and what is false. The atheists quoted earlier relied on their own authority. Will they allow that trust to be tested by reality? If their idea that there is no God is true, it should be reflected in reality. It should make sense logically, and it should be able to be lived out in the real world. Let's put the creation of the universe to the "Two L Test."

How did the universe come into being? There are only three choices: the universe is eternal, the universe created itself, or the universe is created. The first L Test is to ask, "Are any of these options logical?" Is there any evidence that the universe has eternal qualities? Many scientists claim that the universe had a beginning. Also, there is evidence that things are winding down in some measurable degree. In other words, things go from order to disorder. If the universe is winding down, then it makes sense that it must have had a beginning and is not eternal.

The second option would be that the universe created itself. How can something that does not exist, and therefore needs to be created, create itself? The first L Test will not allow for self-creation. If our own science ("what we know") informs our philosophy ("what we don't know"), the question can honestly be asked if either an eternal universe or a self-created universe makes logical sense. Upon what authority will we base our answer? We are left with the third option: the universe is the result of an act of creation. The third option of a created universe is still alive. The first L Test makes logical sense, since it appears to match reality.

The second L Test is whether or not we can live out our conclusion in the real world. In the real world everything that needs to be created also needs a creator. This is true of everything in this natural world. For example, there would be no person wanting a pizza for dinner who would ever find a pizza somewhere that had existed from eternity. Also, no person would simply sit in front of their TV while a pizza created itself out of nothing right before their eyes. As much as a person would desire a delicious pizza, there would be no pizza existing in eternity and no pizza suddenly appearing without a creator. The eternal pizza can pass neither the first L test, nor the second L test -- it makes no logical sense and it cannot be lived-out in the real world.

TRUTH TRUSTED

What if there is a source outside of ourselves that could lead us to truth that can both match reality and also be lived out in the real world? I offer the possibility of a source from which we may find a trustworthy assessment of what is real. That source is God. The God of the Bible is the uncreated, eternal source of all things. Since God is eternal, he does not need to be created. God himself is The Creator. If God is God, then there can be a no more *trustworthy* source for discerning reality. There are three premises upon which we may base our trust that God is the source of all that is true.

The first premise is that God exists as Creator of all things. If God is the Creator of all things, then he must know a few things that we don't know. Could it be that God has revealed some of these things (truth—reality) to us?

Premise # 1—God is Creator of all things.

The second premise is that God has indeed revealed truth to us. His truth may be found in the Bible. Some people may not know much about the Bible or may not have much confidence that they will find truth and reality in the Bible. I would ask them to consider strongly that the Bible is God's revelation to us. God caused the Bible to be written, collected, and preserved so that we might know *his* reality and *his* truth. I would suggest that people start by leaving the door open for the possibility that God has indeed left us with a trust-worthy written account of truth. This leads to the second premise.

Premise # 2—The Bible is God's word to us.

Let's start with two concepts: that there is a God who created all things and that he has given us his word, the Bible. With these two foundational premises in place we can know what is real and what is true. We can move forward in confidence that it is possible to find a good, trustworthy guide for life. Based on the first two premises we come to a third premise.

Premise # 3—We may place our faith in God and in his word, the Bible.

THE QUESTION OF FAITH

What is faith? A Sunday school teacher asked her young students to give her a definition of faith. One eager student stood up and proclaimed, "Faith is believing in something even when you know it is not true." Many people have the mistaken idea that faith is not supposed to make sense. Granted, sometimes we may not have a full understanding of certain things, but the biblical definition of faith demands that our faith be grounded in truth. We are given a definition of faith in the book of Hebrews:

Faith is being sure of what we hope for and certain of what we do not see (Hebrews 11:1).

"Being sure" tells us that there is reality and substance (a reason) for faith. We may not have the completed answer yet, but we have good reason to place our faith that the full answer will arrive one day. There may still be the tension of some unanswered questions or partial details, but we wait patiently—in faith.

Abraham is given as a reliable and trustworthy example of someone who had faith. Abraham received a promise from God. Based on that promise Abraham obeyed and followed God's instructions. Was Abraham's faith based on reality or substance? Yes. His faith was based on the promise of God. Abraham's faith was not without reason. He had good reason for believing. He had the promise of God. The first part of the definition of faith—"being sure of what we hope for"—was lived out by Abraham. If he had claimed that a space alien, or Santa Claus, or the man in the moon had given him the promise, then his faith would have little reason or substance. As we read the account of Abraham from Genesis, chapters 12 to 22, we find that he was visited seven times by God and given powerful promises. Abraham's faith was based on reality and reason.

The second part of the definition of faith states that "faith is being certain of what we do not see." The term "certain" means that there is proof (evidence) for belief. How do we prove that something invisible exists? Courtrooms do it all the time. Facts are proven through evidence of an event that was unseen by any of the members of the jury. The jury makes decisions based on that evidence. There is certainty. The evidence brings faith down to earth. What is *our* evidence? Our evidence is God's word, the Bible.

Hebrews, chapter 11, has been called "the faith chapter." It begins with this strong definition of faith: *"Faith is being sure of what we hope for and certain of what we do not see."* There is not a wishy-washy word in this definition. The definition itself is steeped in meaning and reason. Faith is the act of trusting and then acting on that trust. God's word implies that faith is a good thing and that we are to be commended for our faith. God is alive, and he rewards faith. A few verses later we read:

Without faith it is impossible to please God, because anyone who comes to him must believe that he exists and that he rewards those who earnestly seek him (Hebrews 11:6).

Belief in the existence of God is an essential part of our faith. Another essential part of our faith is the attitude we carry into our search for the truth. Jesus said that the truth will set us free. He made that statement as he was confronted with a group of people who had a contrary attitude towards him. An attitude of faith is crucial for receiving the freedom that Jesus promised. This is what makes the third premise of well-placed faith so important.

Our atheist friends presented a false dichotomy between faith and reason. They claimed that reason (science) is what we know but that faith (philosophy) is what we don't know. What we *must* know is that this is a non-biblical definition of faith. Faith and reason are not to be separated. It was God himself who called to his wayward people, *"Come now, let us REASON together"* (Isaiah 1:18). Jesus was asked what the greatest commandment was in the law. He answered, *"Love the Lord your God with all your heart and with all your soul and with all your MIND"* (Matthew 22:37). Faith and reason go together. We might say, "What God has joined together, let not man separate." We are not to separate faith and reason.

Jesus was the one who said, "The truth will set you free." Taken in context, the truth must be *his* truth. There can be no greater, trustworthy authority for learning the truth that Jesus referred to than the Bible itself. The Bible is the teaching of Jesus. The Bible must be our foundation for truth. It possesses authority that can be trusted to lead us into the Truth that will set us free. When we hold a Bible in our hands we are holding a very trustworthy authority for what is true.

CHALLENGE

IF the God of the Bible is real, *then*, this God should be the source of truth.

IF the God of the Bible is real, *then*, we should be able to know and understand at least some of his truth. The premise is that, since we are made in God's image, we should be able to find much of God's truth that resonates within us. The way God thinks and sees the world should be available to our understanding. God's truth should be reasonable. His truth should make logical sense to us.

TIME OUT

Write out these two verses from Hebrews 11 on a piece of paper:

Faith is being sure of what we hope for and certain of what we do not see (Hebrews 11:1).

Without faith it is impossible to please God, because anyone who comes to him must believe that he exists and that he rewards those who earnestly seek him (Hebrews 11:6).

Memorize them. Carry them with you and pull them out from time to time and meditate upon them. The next time you encounter doubt or discouragement, do not let your faith go bankrupt. Declare Chapter Eleven!—Hebrews chapter eleven.

Your faith will increase as you learn to trust in God's word.

IF the God of the Bible is real, *then*, we should be able to place our faith in his truth.

Truth is not always *"new!"* or *"improved!"* Have you ever noticed how popular TV documentaries about the Bible seem to gravitate toward the sensational and the controversial? These documentaries will focus on questionable topics such as the Shroud of Turin or Jesus' wife. Why not present the tested and plain facts that, over time, have been proven to be trustworthy? The new and the sensational attract more attention. Perhaps TV programmers depend on keeping viewers mesmerized so they will be less tempted to change the channel.

We are challenged to readjust our thinking to realize that the search for truth will not always be as sensational as the latest controversy or the newest scintillating scandal. Truth is bedrock. Truth is old, and, as a result, it will not always be "new." Therefore, we must be willing to exercise discipline and maturity as we work through the facts and weigh them with careful attention. This is not to say that truth is not exciting. It can be the most exciting and life-changing power in a person's life.

Everyone has reasons for believing certain things. We don't have to know everything, but at least we can have good grounds for belief. The chapters that follow were written to add strength and confidence toward a vibrant and living faith in God. Our faith can be based on good evidence. This chapter on faith and truth should help give you confidence that your faith is well placed. The objective of *Christian Basics* is to help people grow ever closer to the one who said, *"I am the truth"* (John 14:6).

A PRAYER FOR YOU

May Jesus give those who take up the challenge of going through these chapters in *Christian Basics* the same experience that the disciples had as they walked with him on the road to Emmaus. *"Were not our hearts burning within us while he talked with us on the road and opened the Scriptures to us?"* (Luke 24:32) They had no idea a study of Scripture and his words could be so exciting. May God open up the Scriptures to you in a new way just as he did to those disciples on the road to Emmaus.

STUDY QUESTIONS

1. What are the three premises for approaching your study of the Bible?

2. How can you explain a worldview that allows for the possibility of a supernatural God?

3. How would you explain to someone the importance of *not* separating faith from reason?

4. How would you explain Hebrews 11:1 and Hebrews 11:6 to someone who had a question about the nature of faith?

5. Read and reread the quote from Jesus from John 8:31–32. How would you explain to someone the truth that Jesus had in mind?

QUESTIONS PEOPLE ASK

■ *Does it show a lack of faith to want faith to be reasonable?*

Genesis 1:26 says that we are created in the image of God. That image may be spoiled by sin, but we still have the ability to reason and think. If reason has no bearing on faith, God would not draw his people to himself with such words as: *"Come let us reason together"* (Isaiah 55:1).

In fact, if faith lacked reason and logic, then why would God even choose to use words at all? Why would God call people to account for his words? Perhaps faith could merely be a person's intuition or feeling. It shouldn't take a very close reading of the Bible to see that God uses language and logic (reason) in his dealings with his people.

The language of God (the Bible) gives us many tangible reasons for faith. Our task is to understand God's ways as they are worked out in human history. We may not always understand his ways fully at first, but we can work toward an understanding. We will discover that both our faith and our reason will grow stronger.

■ *Do I have to enroll in Bible College in order to understand the Bible?*

No. The Bible was written for all to understand. The early believers did not have a Bible college. Scripture is meant to be understood by all. That being said, Bible college and other advanced studies are helpful in enabling people to increase their effectiveness in working with others in a wide variety of ways.

Some people do not read or study the Bible due to the false notion that they must have a biblical degree. They may give all the responsibility to the pastor or the experts. Every believer is called to study God's word. Some people choose to go deeper in order to increase their effectiveness in working with others and to answer the call on their lives. The Bible was written, compiled, and preserved so that all might come to the knowledge of the truth.

■ *I often struggle with lack of faith. What can I do to strengthen my faith?*

The illustration has often been given that a believer's life can be seen as a table with four legs: The Bible—Prayer/Worship—Fellowship—Service. If any of these legs are weak or missing, there will be imbalance. It would be good to make an appraisal of any of these four areas to see if there might be something missing.

Are you engaged in disciplined Bible study? Do you take to heart God's word by meditation and memorization? Are you involved in prayer and worship? Are prayer and worship a vital part of your life? Do you attend a Bible-based church? Are you involved in the lives of others for mutual encouragement in the faith? Are you involved in some kind of service, no matter how small it may seem?

The four areas listed are by no means meant to be some kind of mechanical and dry method to produce faith, but they are a good place to start. God is alive, and he will help you as you seek him. Your faith will grow stronger as you get involved in the teaching of the Bible which is given to all believers.

Chapter Two

THE BIBLE

KEY POINTS

- How the Bible was put together and preserved
- How the rules of literature apply to the Bible
- The role of the Holy Spirit in the inspiration of the Bible
- How to read the Bible using the normal rules of language

When you hold a Bible in your hand, you are holding a miracle. Stop for a minute and think about the implications of this. Jesus said that if we hold to his teaching we would know the truth. The Bible is *the* central source of authority for knowing the teachings of Jesus. The Bible is a book that can be trusted. The Bible is the best and most trustworthy source for obtaining a correct view of the Christian faith.

ATTITUDE ALERT

Some people hold to the idea that there is no God or at least that there is no supernatural intervention by God in the affairs of human beings. This can lead to an anti-supernatural bias that can divest the Bible of credibility and power. This is an ALERT to bring to light a presupposition that might prevent a well-balanced and fair study of the Bible. We all live with presuppositions in the way we think about the world. We see the world through these presuppositions. It is normal. Please give this second chapter a fair reading and then decide if those people holding to an anti-supernatural presupposition are justified in doing so.

The issue of the supernatural nature of the Bible is a very important point to consider. Many of the controversies over the reliability and validity of the Bible can be better understood if the philosophy and presuppositions undergirding the arguments can be recognized. Some people have a philosophy, or worldview, that will not allow for the supernatural. Others have a worldview that will allow for the supernatural.

You are invited to give this second chapter on the Bible a fair reading with an *attitude* of openness. Please consider the possibility that there might be a miracle-working God behind the inspiration and the preservation of the very Bible we can now hold in our hands.

Section One

THE MIRACLE OF THE BIBLE

The first verse in the Bible says, *"In the beginning God created the heavens and the earth"* (Genesis 1:1). If this first verse can be believed, then it follows that we can also believe it is possible for God to intervene in his creation. If God can intervene in his creation, then it is possible that God could cause a book to be written and preserved over a long period of time. *If* God could create the universe, *then* he could also easily cause a book to be constructed under his watchful eye to be accurate and trustworthy. Let's begin our study of the Bible with this idea in mind: the Bible is both a supernaturally *inspired* and a supernaturally *preserved* book. When you hold a Bible in your hands, you are holding a miracle.

■ THE MIRACLE OF CONSISTENCY

The Bible tells one totally integrated, continuous story from beginning to end. From Genesis to Revelation there is a continuous story of God reaching out to his creation. It tells, with complete harmony within itself, one consistent and continuous account of God's involvement in human history. The Bible shows how God relates to his creation from the very beginning all the way to the end of time.

What makes the consistency of the Bible so amazing (and miraculous) is that the Bible is not just one book. The Bible is made up of sixty-six books. Each one is in agreement with the other. Furthermore, the Bible was not written by only one person. It was written by more than forty different authors over a time span of 1,500 years. It was written on three different continents and in three different languages.

Imagine if you were given the task of writing a book that was to be as profound as the Bible. It would have to speak about many controversial subjects regarding life and death, history, poetry and predictive prophecy. It would have to be written in complete harmony with itself and then fit together as a complete unit. Keep in mind that this project must span 1,500 years. How would you start? For anyone to tackle such a grand project would be an absolute impossibility. Who would be around to write for 1,500 years (never mind spreading it over three continents and three different languages)? The point is that it would be beyond the realm of human possibility. Nobody could do it—nobody but God. It has been said,"The Bible is not such a book a man would write if he could, or could write if he would."

The miracle of the Bible is that it is not a book of human origin. It has the mark of having been written by a supernatural author—God. This is what we mean when we say that the Bible is *inspired*. There are two very important verses from the New Testament that speak of the inspiration of the Bible:

All Scripture is God-breathed and is useful for teaching, rebuking, correcting and training in righteousness, so that the man of God may be thoroughly equipped for every good work (2 Timothy 3:16–17).

Above all, you must understand that no prophecy of Scripture came about by the prophet's own interpretation. For prophecy never had its origin in the will of man, but men spoke from God as they were carried along by the Holy Spirit (2 Peter 1:20–21).

As you read and contemplate the meaning of these two quotes from the Bible, please notice how much God has had his hand in the writing of the Bible. Contemplate also how God has used certain specially chosen men and, through them, caused his words to be recorded and then preserved all the way to this present time.

TIME OUT

Take time out in your study to try to memorize these two passages of Scripture. Bible memorization is a practice that is part of every believer's life. These Scriptures answer the question: Where does it say that the Bible is inspired? File them mentally as being in 2 Timothy and 2 Peter. By remembering the question and the location in the Bible you will be able to encourage your own faith and you will also be able to encourage others over your lifetime.

Write out 2 Timothy 3:16–17 and 2 Peter 1:20–21 fully on little note cards and carry them around with you until they become a part of your life. Memorize them.

The Bible is an amazing book to have been written over such a long period of time and with so much potential for contradiction. Yet, it tells one complete and harmonious story. There is no other book (66 books) in existence like it in the world. This miraculous consistency is one of the reasons that the Bible can be considered to be an inspired and infallible source for the Christian faith.

■ THE MIRACLE OF SURVIVAL

It is very important to know that when we say that the Bible is inspired and infallible, we are speaking of the original writings, not the copies. The original writings have long since disappeared, and we are now left with copies of the originals. How are we to judge the truth and accuracy of the copies compared to the original writings? This is a crucial question. Please be aware that the question of the accuracy and the reliability of copying is not only a problem for the Bible, but for all ancient literature as well. We have no original manuscripts of any ancient writing, only copies. There is an answer to this problem that will actually serve to strengthen our faith in the reliability of the Bible.

It is amazing that the Bible we hold in our hands is writing that has been preserved for more than 3,000 years in the Old Testament and for nearly 2,000 years in the New Testament. Part of the reason for this is that God himself raised up a people who would be caretakers of his word. These caretakers were the Jews. As far back as the time of Moses we can read where God told Moses to write down the words that he was given (Exodus 17:14). The Ten Commandments were to be kept in the Ark of the Covenant (Exodus 25:16). God's words were a crucial and vital part of the lives of the Jews. Later, the kings were commanded to write down their own copies of the law so they might follow it closely (Deuteronomy 17:18–20). Keeping and preserving God's word was the central issue to God and his people. It was by no accident that the Jews have been called "the people of the Book."

The ancient Jews were a culture of memory. God's word was memorized and passed on with incredible accuracy. A deeper look into the Old Testament will reveal that much of it was written in such a way as to foster retention. Parallelisms, alliterations, and plays on words abound. It is not easy to carry these literary devices over into other language translations, but it can be seen how these devices were used to facilitate memory and retention over many generations.

In the transmission of the texts there was a very unique group of people who religiously took on the challenge of accurate copying. These were the scribes. They treated their work as a holy undertaking. They counted the words, and they counted the lines on each page (or scroll section). Even the letters were counted. Errors were to be feared. After all, they were engaged in the transmission of the holy word of God who himself commanded in, Deuteronomy 12:32, that no one add or subtract from his words.

The Bible was indeed copied with the utmost care and precision. The common criticisms used to discount the accuracy of the transmission of the Bible are often weak. A common criticism using the old "telephone" party game is an example. In the telephone game the message passed on was intentionally kept a secret and divergent messages were expected and enjoyed. The scribes were not playing a game, and the message was not kept secret. Their copies were under the scrutiny of rigorous checks and counter-checks.

To help illustrate how well the manuscripts were copied, let's take a quick look at a comparison of the ancient writings of Plato and Aristotle with the writings of the Bible. We do not have the original manuscripts of Plato or Aristotle. It is interesting that the accuracy of the copies of these ancient works is seldom questioned.

Plato and Aristotle lived around 350 B.C. The earliest manuscripts from their works range from about A.D. 900 to A.D. 1100. There are only a handful of these oldest copies in existence. Few people doubt the accuracy and reliability of these copies even though there is a time span averaging about 1,300 years between the original writings and the copies that now exist. The confidence scholars enjoy for the copies of Plato and Aristotle should be a tremendous encouragement for the readers of the Bible. When we compare the manuscript evidence of the Bible, you will see that our confidence in the Bible is not without good reason.

Let's look at a comparative example from the Old Testament book of Isaiah. Up until the discovery of the Dead Sea Scrolls the earliest copy of Isaiah was dated at approximately A.D. 900. Since Isaiah prophesied around 700 B.C. this would leave a time gap of 1,600 years. A copy of Isaiah was found in a cave near the Dead Sea in 1948. This copy can be dated to the year 100 B.C. This discovery enabled the experts to view something extremely rare: manuscripts of the same books that were separated by 1,000 years (with no copies in between). Upon comparison there was very little difference except in some spelling and other minor details. This comparison rendered the book of Isaiah to be considered trustworthy. This should serve as an amazing example of the reliability of the Old Testament. Remember, there was a clearly documented 1,000 year gap. This is tangible, physical evidence of trustworthy copying.

Jesus placed the utmost confidence in the Old Testament:

And beginning with Moses and all the Prophets, he explained to them what was said in all the Scriptures concerning himself (Luke 24:27).

I tell you the truth, until heaven and earth disappear, not the smallest letter, not the least stroke of a pen, will by any means disappear from the law until everything is accomplished (Matthew 5:18).

It is obvious from the mouth of Jesus himself that he had no trouble trusting in the reliability of the Scriptures. Again and again he called people to account based on what was written. We have essentially the same Old Testament today that was in existence at the time of Christ. Jesus' own opinion of the Scriptures should never be forgotten in our study of the topic of the reliability of the Bible.

When the New Testament is considered the manuscript evidence skyrockets. Most of the New Testament was written between the years A.D. 50–90. The earliest complete copy is from around A.D. 300 (although partial copies and fragments are older). This would create a gap of 200 years that is much smaller than that for other ancient manuscripts. There are around 5,000 copies in existence along with thousands more in languages other than the original Greek. If we add to this the many notes and quotes taken from the New Testament that can be gleaned from other ancient writings, we then have an overwhelming wealth of material to help us check on the accuracy of what we hold in our hands today. Compare all this to what we have in the examples of Plato and Aristotle, and you can begin to see that our high opinion of the Bible is reasonable.

Biblical scholar Bruce Metzger commented as he was discussing the manuscript evidence for the writings of Homer and other authors of ancient literature as it compared to the biblical manuscript evidence.

> In contrast with these figures, the textual critic of the New Testament is embarrassed by the wealth of his material. Furthermore, the work of many an ancient author has been preserved only in manuscripts which date from the Middle Ages (sometimes in the late Middle Ages), far removed from the time at which he lived and wrote. On the contrary, the time between the composition of the books of the New Testament and the earliest extant copies is relatively brief. [1]

It is fully scientific to say that we can trust the authority of the Scriptures. The manuscript evidence is tangible testimony to the miracle of the survival of the Bible. The consistency of the sixty-six books in our Bible is a miracle that we can hold in our hands.

■ THE MIRACLE OF PROPHECY

What is prophecy? It is two things: (1) the foretelling of events before they happen, and (2) the forth-telling of God's message, that is, speaking for God. We will be concerned here with the foretelling/ prediction of future events.

It is interesting just how easily most people accept the idea of prophecy. Every year the magazine stands are full of predictions by all of the latest soothsayers. The tales of Nostradamus and his prognostications hold people in awe. Every year there seems to be a new prophet predicting that the world will end. It is important to know

---

1   Bruce Metzger, *The Text of the New Testament* (New York: Oxford University Press, 1968), 34.

that, according to the Bible, they all miss the mark. First, most of these predictions do not come to pass. Secondly, most of them are vague or they concern mundane topics with little effect upon history. History marches on without being impacted or enlightened by these predictions.

Bible prophecy is set apart from common prophecy due to the demands of an extreme standard. The biblical standard is much higher because the events predicted must come to pass with one hundred percent accuracy. The mistake many people make is to place the common worldly standard of the "anything goes" prophecy upon the Bible. There is the popular idea that prophecy can be defined as rather loose predictions that may or may not come to pass as predicted. This hit-or-miss variety of making predictions is a different definition from what constitutes biblical prophecy. The Bible explicitly and strictly allows for no error.

One time in Israel's history God reassured the people that, once Moses was no longer with them, he would send them prophets just like Moses. How would they know that the prophet was actually speaking for God?

You may say to yourselves, "How can we know when a message has not been spoken by the LORD?" If what a prophet proclaims in the name of the LORD does not take place or come true, that is a message the LORD has not spoken. That prophet has spoken presumptuously. Do not be afraid of him (Deuteronomy 18:21–22).

It should stand to reason that anyone coming forward as a prophet of God would only speak of things that would come true. The premise is that God makes no mistakes. This is a very stringent test that we must still apply today to those claiming to be speaking for God in the realm of predictive prophecy. The demands of such a test would eliminate a lot of what is going on in contemporary prophetic circles and rescue people from harmful deception. This test also directs a bright light on the prophecies that are already contained in the Bible for all to read. The biblical test of prophecy is one hundred percent accuracy.

The study of prophecy in the Bible is exciting. It not only strengthens our faith, but it also helps prove that the Bible is not a man-made book. Predicting the future is the province of God. Anyone else who has tried to predict the future has met with failure. We must not let this point pass without recognizing its profound importance. Only God can predict the future, and his predictions are recorded in the Bible as *his* word:

I am God, and there is no other. I am God, and there is none like me. I make known the end from the beginning, from ancient times, what is still to come (Isaiah 46:9–10).

There are many prophecies in the Bible that were fulfilled exactly as predicted. The more your study of the Bible deepens, the more of these prophecies you will discover. Your faith will grow stronger as a result. There are prophecies concerning many foreign nations other than Israel, prophecies concerning kings and queens, prophecies about world events, and prophecies about the coming of the Messiah. Biblical prophecies are not of the parlor game variety. They have a profound effect upon the history of the world.

As an example, let's look at a few regarding Jesus. There were many prophecies about Jesus written hundreds of years before he came into the world. Here are just a few examples from the New Testament book of Matthew:

■ The prophet Nathan told King David that a descendent of David's would be king forever. The reign of every other king ended naturally, including David's. Not so with this king. This prophecy was recorded in 2 Samuel 7:12–14 and fulfilled about 1000 years later. " . . . *Jesus Christ, son of David*" (Matthew 1:1). Jesus Christ will reign forever.

- Matthew quoted from the prophet Isaiah, who lived around 700 B.C., and related one of Isaiah's prophecies (Isaiah 7:14) directly to the birth of Jesus:

"All this took place to fulfill what the Lord had said though the prophet: 'The virgin will be with child and will give birth to a son, and they will call him Immanuel'" (Matthew 1:22–23).

- When the magi came to visit the baby Jesus they first came to Herod who then asked the religious leaders where the Christ was to be born. They answered:

"In Bethlehem in Judea, for this is what the prophet has written: 'But you, Bethlehem, in the land of Judah, are by no means least among the rulers of Judah; for out of you will come a ruler who will be the shepherd of my people Israel'" (Matthew 2:5–6).

They quoted a well-known prophecy from the prophet Micah (Micah 5:2) who lived at least 600 years before the events foretold took place. The Bible is full of prophetic statements about Jesus Christ. Read the words of Jesus himself as he commented on the prophecies that were concerning him:

He said to them, "How foolish you are, and slow of heart to believe all that the prophets have spoken! Did not the Christ have to suffer these things and then enter his glory?" And beginning with Moses and all the Prophets, he explained to them what was said in all the Scriptures concerning himself (Luke 24:25–27).

When Luke wrote, *"Moses and all the Prophets,"* it was a common way of referring to all of the Old Testament. Jesus reaffirmed this fact in Luke 24:44. This should help confirm the fact that many things were foretold about Jesus in the Old Testament. Furthermore, Jesus wanted people to be aware of this fact. I would love to have been at that Bible study as Jesus expounded upon the Old Testament Scriptures that referred to him.

Bible prophecy makes for very interesting study. There is no other book like the Bible containing hundreds of specific prophecies that can be proven historically accurate. This is a very important point that gives further credence to the miraculous nature of the Bible.

Consider biblical prophecy as God having left his "calling cards" throughout history. These calling cards function as a time capsule locked within historic events. No one can go back and change what was written. They are scattered throughout the Bible. The fact that these prophecies were written down for posterity places God's word to scrutiny for all to see.

Beyond Bible prophecy there are also many prophetic events that occurred in Israel's history that foreshadow the nature and the ministry of the Messiah. These events have been called types and shadows, or prefigurations, of Christ. For example, there is the tabernacle and priesthood system. A careful study of this sacrificial system will unlock astounding portraits of Christ. Another place for fruitful study is the Feasts of the LORD. The Passover, Pentecost, and the Feast of Tabernacles all have prophetic implications concerning Jesus Christ. There are many more that may be studied, such as the manna, the rock, and the bronze serpent in the wilderness.

These are the things that set the Bible apart from being just an ordinary book. It is a book directly inspired by God. Since it is a book from God with a message from God, we have every reason to believe that the message it contains has the power to change lives.

■ THE MIRACLE OF POWER

The Bible is a book of power. But, it is not a book of enchantment like a magic talisman or a lucky charm. God's word is alive by the power of the Holy Spirit to bring change in the lives of those who put their trust in Christ. Since God is alive, we believe he can, and does, work through his word:

For the word of God is living and active. Sharper than any double-edged sword, it penetrates even to dividing soul and spirit, joints and marrow; it judges the thoughts and attitudes of the heart. Nothing in all creation is hidden from God's sight. Everything is laid bare before the eyes of him to whom we must give account. (Hebrews 4:12–13).

The Bible has the power to answer the ultimate and essential questions that have plagued humanity from the beginning of history: Who are we? Where are we going? Why are we here?

The Bible has power because it is designed to lead people to Christ. When people meet Jesus, lives are changed. The Bible is ultimately about Jesus. *". . . the testimony of Jesus is the spirit of prophecy"* (Revelation 19:10). Jesus alluded to this when he was berating the religious leaders for rejecting him. *"You diligently study the Scriptures . . . These are the Scriptures that testify about me, yet you refuse to come to me to have life"* (John 5:39–40). Jesus was referring to one of the main purposes of the Scriptures. Scripture is meant to lead people to Christ so that they can enter into a life-changing relationship with God through him.

The source of the spiritual power that is inherent in the Bible is from the Holy Spirit. (We will look more deeply into the person and work of the Holy Spirit in the sixth chapter of *Christian Basics*). We must be aware that the power, or leverage, to change a person's life comes from the Holy Spirit. The Holy Spirit will use the word of God. The Bible is a spiritual book inspired by the Holy Spirit. All people reading Scripture must have the supernatural help of the Holy Spirit. Part of this mystery is explained in the following passage:

The man without the Spirit does not accept the things that come from the Spirit of God, for they are foolishness to him, and he cannot understand them, because they are spiritually discerned. (1 Corinthians 2:14).

Hopefully, being aware of the necessity for spiritual help in reading and understanding the message contained in the Bible will cause you to read it with a new sense of humility. Humility mixed with faith can go a long way to paving the way for the power of God's word to penetrate deeply into the heart of each sincere reader.

In review, the four main reasons for considering the Bible a miracle you can hold in your hand are:

1. The miracle of consistency—God's inspiration down through time.
2. The miracle of survival—God's providence in protection and preservation.
3. The miracle of prophecy—God's omniscience in knowing the future.
4. The miracle of power—God's will in drawing and nurturing a people for himself.

We have looked at the miracle of the Bible. Considering all the facts presented, to call the Bible "a miracle that we can hold in our hands" is not an overstatement. Now let's look at another feature of the Bible.

Section Two

THE SUFFICIENCY OF THE BIBLE

The Bible is sufficient in all matters dealing with the faith and practice of the Christian faith. In other words, other than the Bible, no other writings or any other human organization may serve as the measure of what is ultimately true and valid pertaining to Christian doctrine and practice. The Bible is the sole authority. The authority of Scripture trumps all.

Questions often come up concerning other religious writings. How can we ignore all the other religious writings and cling only to the Bible? Isn't that being unfair to all the other religions in the world? Questions such as these force us to take a close look at why we view the Bible as the sole sufficient source of revelation about God and the Christian faith.

An understanding of the concept of "canon" is important. The word "canon" comes from an old word that means "cane." A reed cane would often be used as a measuring rod in the ancient world. Canon is the term used for writings that "measure up" as worthy of being Scripture. All writings had to fit certain criteria. If they passed the tests for canon (measuring rod), they were accepted.

THE TEST FOR THE OLD TESTAMENT

The canon of the Old Testament was not in question in Jesus' day. The Jews themselves had settled the question at least one hundred years before the birth of Christ. Many times other writings were considered, but were rejected and not added to the Old Testament. When Jesus referred to "the Law of Moses, the Prophets and the Psalms" he was referring to the Old Testament that is essentially the same as we have today.

There are two major tests for all Scripture. The first test is found in Deuteronomy 13 and refers to orthodoxy:

If a prophet, or one who foretells by dreams, appears among you and announces to you a miraculous sign or wonder, and if the sign or wonder of which he has spoken takes place, and he says, "Let us follow other gods" (gods you have not known) "and let us worship them," you must not listen to the words of that prophet or dreamer (Deuteronomy 13:1–4).

It is very important to notice that even if a person were to perform a miracle, yet taught things that failed to line up with previously accepted truth, that teaching would be considered false. It would be very tempting to allow false teaching to override true teaching if it was accompanied by a miracle.

All teaching and writing that is to be considered Scripture must conform to what has been accepted previously. A simple example of the principle of orthodoxy would be that the God of Abraham, Isaac, and Jacob would not reveal to one of his true prophets that there were many gods. We have already been instructed that there is only *one* God. No writing could come later and contradict this and at the same time be considered Scripture. It would be rejected based on the principle of orthodoxy as declared in Deuteronomy 13. It would not pass the test of canon.

The second test for Scripture is related to predictive prophecy. God's people would need to know how they could trust future prophets once Moses was no longer with them. How could they be certain that a future prophet may or may not be legitimate?

You may say to yourselves, "How can we know when a message has not been spoken by the LORD?" If what a prophet proclaims in the name of the LORD does not take place or come true, that is a message the LORD has not spoken. Do not be afraid of him (Deuteronomy 18:21–22).

It is good to think for a while about the potential impact of the principles contained in Deuteronomy 13:1–4 and 18:21–22.

- Deuteronomy 13   All teaching must be in total harmony with what was taught in the past.

- Deuteronomy 18   If a prophet's prediction failed to come to pass, he would be, by God's own standards, a false prophet.

Since these two restrictive guidelines were followed, it was very difficult for false teaching to creep into the Bible during its formation. God raised up prophets to exhort his people to adhere to the principles and laws in Scripture. The Scriptures were to be the standard to guide them.

THE TEST FOR THE NEW TESTAMENT

The New Testament also had to meet the guidelines of both Deuteronomy 13 and 18. Not just any writing could be called Scripture. There had to be certain qualifications regarding authorship, and there could be no errors in history or other relevant facts.

It might sound like a strange concept at first, but the church did not *proclaim* which books belonged in the New Testament as much as they were *discovered*. The books that promoted faith and edification had a way of rising above all others. They eventually became universally recognized, while the less influential writings fell out of use. This is not to say that there wasn't much discussion and struggle over certain books. By the late fourth century the issue was largely settled. We can confidently say that the books we now have in our New Testament were the result of the most careful and meticulous consideration.

THE CLOSED CANON

The concept of the closed canon means that no new Scripture can be added to what we now have. The canon was closed shortly after the last of the original Apostles died. Even though it took a few hundred years for the issue to be settled, the Apostles had the final authority. There is now no one who has the authority to speak for God and then have it recorded as Scripture. Nothing *has* been added for 2,000 years and nothing *will* be added.

Once the principle of the closed canon is understood, it might make for interesting study to see what was rejected as Scripture. There is a collection of writings that were not included in the Old Testament. They are called the "Apocrypha." Although the Roman Catholic Bible contains these books, both the Jewish Scriptures and Protestant Bibles have excluded them. Anyone is free to read the apocryphal books. They are not forbidden reading, but they are not considered Scripture.

There were also writings that were not included in the New Testament. The believing community rejected them on the same grounds as the Old Testament canon.

The principle of the closed canon and the absolute authority of Scripture is a crucial one today. Many religious organizations and cult leaders have been able to garner authority for themselves in direct violation of this principle and have led many people astray. This should make us aware of the dangers involved in adding to, or subtracting from, the word of God as contained in our Bible.

OUR RESPONSIBILTY

It is very important to know that God has given the individual believer the responsibility to discern what conforms to Scriptural truth. We are not to leave it up to an outside authority to make these decisions for us. This is not to say that we should not be advised or instructed, but the ultimate responsibility lies with each believer. Jesus said:

For false Christs and false prophets will appear and perform great signs and miracles to deceive even the elect—if that were possible (Matthew 24:24).

Jesus gave us this solemn warning. It is a warning we cannot ignore. How are we to discern between a false teacher and a true teacher? There have been many leaders with overpowering charisma who have led many people into danger. Jesus said that even if they performed miraculous signs and miracles, they still could be false teachers. Most people would have little reluctance attributing divine status to a leader who was able to display a miracle for all to see. We've been warned that even a miracle was not to be allowed to set the standard for truth. The standard is the Bible.

Let's look at three examples of how we are to discern truth from error:

■ The Example of the Bereans

The apostle Paul was traveling from city to city preaching the gospel. He had difficulty in Thessalonica. Many of the town's people managed to cause such a ruckus that Paul barely escaped with his life. As he entered the city of Berea, he began to preach the gospel there, but this time with different results:

Now the Bereans were of more noble character than the Thessalonians, for they received the message with great eagerness and examined the Scriptures every day to see if what Paul said was true (Acts 17:11).

Paul was not offended when the Bereans checked out his teachings to see if they were in line with the whole of Scripture. They applied the test of Deuteronomy 13 to make sure everything Paul taught was in harmony with Scripture.

Many people have the false idea that when a famous (or not so famous) Bible teacher gets behind a pulpit, we are not supposed to check out what is being taught. Some might even say that it would be judgmental to do so. However, we are supposed to judge all teaching and preaching in the light of what has already been revealed to us plainly in the Bible. Paul commended the Bereans for doing just that. Even the great Apostle Paul placed himself under this same abiding principle. It should follow that any trustworthy preacher or Bible teacher would want to do the same.

■ The Example of the Galatians

A very important section in the letter to the church in Galatia quite powerfully reinforces the necessity of discerning truth. Paul began his letter to the Galatians by taking them to task for allowing themselves to be wrongly influenced by false teachers:

I am so astonished that you are so quickly deserting the one who called you by the grace of Christ and are turning to a different gospel—which is really no gospel at all. Evidently some people are throwing you into confusion and are trying to pervert the gospel of Christ. But even if we or an angel from heaven should preach a gospel other than the one we preached to you, let him be eternally condemned! As we have already said, so now I say again: If anybody is preaching to you a gospel other than what you accepted, let him be eternally condemned (Galatians 1:6–9).

Paul placed the responsibility of determining true and false teaching squarely on the believers themselves. They were to be so trained and well versed in the Scriptures that they would be able to detect false teaching. Notice also that Paul also placed himself under this same scrutiny. Paul could have very well pulled rank if he wanted to do so because of his unique calling as an Apostle. However, Paul did not exclude himself from the same standard that applies to all. All teachers would be wise to take a lesson from the great Apostle Paul and submit their teachings to the authority of Scripture.

Paul even included supernatural visitations from an angel into his warning. How many people today would fall all over themselves to adhere to most any teaching if a real, visible angel taught it? It would make headlines and be on every talk show and news program. The whole world would be following the teaching from this angel. Paul cautioned us to be wary of supernatural visitations that might be false. Even teachings from an angel from heaven must be under the same strict guidelines. All teaching must line up with what has been previously revealed in the Bible—as prescribed in Deuteronomy 13:1–4. There should be no exceptions. Most cults with dangerous teachings would collapse if these guidelines were followed today.

■ Example from 1 John

The warning in John's first letter is very powerful and direct. When the entire context of the Bible is considered, it becomes evident that one of the common recurring themes is that there has always been the danger of false prophets. The same is true to this day:

Dear friends, do not believe every spirit, but test the spirits to see whether they are from God, because many false prophets have gone out into the world (1 John 4:1).

No teacher, no preacher, no evangelist, or any organization is exempt from having their teachings tested for biblical orthodoxy. All must be subject to the objective test of sound biblical truth. Jesus said that many false prophets would arise. Jesus gave this warning 2,000 years ago. The warning still stands today. This has been an ongoing, ever-present problem for God's people since the beginning of time itself.

TIME OUT

In review, the two major tests for biblical truth come from the Old Testament. First, we have Deuteronomy 13:1–4. This is the test for orthodoxy (straight teaching). Orthodoxy is teaching that lines up with what has been previously revealed in the Bible. Then there is Deuteronomy 18:21–22. This is the test of one hundred percent accuracy in predictive prophecy.

These two tests were reinforced in the New Testament: Luke 24:25–27; Acts 17:11; Galatians 1:6–9; and 1 John 4:1.

■ First—Memorize where these can be located in the Bible.

■ Second—Be very familiar with the principle of the test for biblical orthodoxy.

Memorize this chart:

Old Testament Tests:	Deuteronomy 13:1–4
	18:21–22
New Testament Examples:	Luke 24:25–27
	Acts 17:11
	Galatians 1:6–9
	1 John 4:1

Section Three

THE PROPER READING OF THE BIBLE

Sometimes there is confusion due to the fact that the Bible has been interpreted in so many different ways. Once the common rules for interpreting language is understood, much of the confusion disappears. Four major themes form the guidelines for proper reading of the Bible.

■ The Language of the Bible Is Clear

The Bible was not written for elite scholarly theologians. It was written for the regular people of the day. This does not mean that we do not need some help in understanding certain passages. There are some difficult portions of Scripture that may require some assistance. However, the implication of biblical clarity is that the language allows most people to grasp its basic teachings. It is dangerous to think that there are secret codes or deep hidden messages that can only be discerned by those who are spiritually gifted in some mysterious way. We are not supposed to have an unhealthy dependence on any other person or organization for interpretation. The Apostle John wrote the following as a warning:

I am writing these things to you about those who are trying to lead you astray. As for you, the anointing you received from him remains in you, and you do not need anyone to teach you. (1 John 2:26–27).

The Bible declares that God has given the church gifted teachers, but John is warning us about the danger of abdicating our responsibility to read the Bible for ourselves. Many people have allowed certain leaders and/or organizations to twist the plain meaning of Scripture. The consequences have often been tragic. We also must be careful not to use the few difficulties that do exist in the Bible as an excuse for not reading it. The principle of the clarity of the language of the Bible is that the plain meaning is generally clear for all to read and understand.

What about the things that are difficult to understand? Anyone who takes up the challenge of studying the Bible will encounter diffi- cult teachings. If God told you 10,000 things that were absolutely true and understandable, couldn't you trust him for the three or four things that you do not yet understand? Sometimes in our Bible study we may have trouble with certain passages, only to find a suitable solution at a later time. There may even be some biblical problems that will not be solved until we see Jesus face to face. However, we can trust him for what we do know.

■ The Literal Method of Interpretation

The literal method of interpretation means that we interpret the Bible according to the normal rules of language common for all literature. In other words, we do not reserve a separate formula for the Bible and then utilize another set of rules for all other literature. To read the Bible while neglecting the normal rules of literature robs the lan- guage of the Bible of its intended meaning and leads to many errors. The Bible was written with all the rules of language that human beings have used throughout literary history. The literal method is the same method that we use when we read the daily newspaper or any other piece of literature. In fact, we use the literal method of interpretation in everyday life without even being aware of it. This is the normal way that language works.

Commentaries written by sports writers make for an interesting case study in the literal approach. The following is a quote from a sports reporter as he wrote about the woes the San Diego Chargers after their humiliating loss to the Kansas City Chiefs. The headline and story read as follows:

SINKING (GLUB) INTO HUMILIATION (GLUB, GLUB)

"This one didn't carry enough lifeboats. And, somewhere not far away, I thought I heard a band playing the Chargers Give Up Song over the whine of overused bilge pumps. There may have been a last, desperate fight by the Chargers to remain afloat last week, when they managed to hang on to the log that was the Kansas City Chiefs, but they went down for good yesterday" *(S.D. Union/Tribune,* Nick Canepa, 12–4-00).

No reasonable person would take this article in a strictly wooden, literal sense. To do so would be absurd and definitely not the plain meaning intended by the author. Instead, readers automatically employ the literal sense, that is, they would rightly recognize the figures of speech, hyperboles, metaphors and idioms that are particular to football fans (and to creative sports writers).

The same can be said of the Bible. For example, there are descriptions of God having us under the protective shelter of his wings. The normal use of the literal method should cause us to easily recognize that this is figurative language. It would be an error to think that God actually has wings. There are times when certain authors have used poetry, historical narrative, and other genres of literature. All of these genres have nuances that help make literature interesting and memorable. These are the nuances that must be recognized when reading the Bible just as they need to be recognized by any intelligent reader of the newspaper.

■ The Rule of Context

The first rule of context is that individual words get their meaning from the context in which they are placed. It is a mistake to assign a meaning to a word separated from the text that surrounds it. For example, the word "trunk" can have a multitude of meanings until it is read in its context. The context will determine the correct meaning. The word "trunk" will mean something different to a car salesman, a world traveler, a tree trimmer and an elephant trainer.

Many people have made grave mistakes in biblical interpretation because they have allowed themselves, or someone else, to give meaning to biblical words out of context.

The second rule of context is to check a small portion of Scripture against the whole of Scripture. A few verses taken out of context can be twisted to mean something that may contradict the whole context of the Bible. This is a common error and has led to many difficulties. The extreme cases, for example, would be the teachings of Jim Jones that led to the Jonestown disaster in 1978 and the teachings of David Koresh that led to the Waco tragedy in 1993. A review of their teachings would easily show that they led their followers astray by the misuse of Scripture.

The rules of context are an important component in properly reading the Bible. People have been deceived by teaching that they would otherwise have recognized as false had they taken the time to properly apply the rule of context.

■ The Rule of Faith

It is common to hear skeptics say that faith is what we don't know, but science is what we do know. This suggests that there is no faith in science and no knowledge in faith. It is unfortunate that many people adhere to this false definition of faith. To the skeptic, faith is not reasonable. By *their* definition, faith is supposed to be unreasonable. This is *not* the biblical definition of faith.

The Bible gives us the proper definition of faith:

"Faith is being sure of what we hope for and certain of what we do not see" (Hebrews 11:1).

Being *sure* means that we have enough proof to win our trust. We have a new reality opened up for us that creates a substantial basis for believing. Being *certain* implies that we have evidence to back up our certainty. This evidence serves as our proof.

Reading the Bible in faith means that we approach our reading with an active, committed belief. We believe that there is a God who has given us his word, and his word can be trusted. This doesn't mean that we cannot have doubts and questions, but it will mean that we will come to the Bible believing that God is alive and that he will speak to us through his word with the help of the Holy Spirit. Therefore, we read the Bible with an element of trust and faith. There is, after all, plenty of trustworthy evidence for such a faith.

The late D. L. Moody once said that he prayed for faith and thought that someday faith would come down and strike him like lightning. However, faith did not seem to come. One day he read in the tenth chapter of Romans that *"Faith comes by hearing—hearing by the word of God."* He had closed his Bible and prayed for faith. Now he opens his Bible and studies it deeply. His faith kept growing for the rest of his life.

We can listen to the Bible being read. We can read the Bible for ourselves. We can study the Scriptures, meditate, and memorize the Bible. All of these will cause our faith to grow.

Please review

There are four principles for a proper reading of the Bible

1. The writing in the Bible is clear.

2. The same literary principles apply to the Bible as to all literature.

3. The rule of context must be employed.

4. The rule of faith that we have ample proof and evidence in which to place our trust.

CONCLUSION

It is sad to think of how many Bible-believing Christians know so little about the Bible. The Bible is the word of God. The Bible is very much like the miracle of the manna that was given to the children of Israel in the wilderness. The manna was God's provision to give strength and nourishment for his people. For those who belong to Jesus Christ today, the word of God is manna from the Holy Spirit. Let the exhortation from C. H. Mackintosh lead us to a deep hunger for God's word:

> If I sincerely desire to grow in the divine life—if I am earnestly breathing after an extension of God's kingdom within, I shall, without doubt, seek continuously that character of nourishment which is designed of God to promote my spiritual growth. This is plain. A man's acts are always the truest index of his desires and purposes. Hence, if I find a professing Christian neglecting his Bible, yet finding abundance of time— yea, some of his choicest hours—for the newspaper, I can be at no loss to decide as to the true condition of his soul. I am sure he cannot be spiritual—cannot be feeding upon, living for, or witnessing to, Christist. [2]

STUDY QUESTIONS

1. What are some clear Scripture references that speak of the divine inspiration of the Bible?

2. Where does the Bible record Jesus' own words regarding the authority of Scripture?

3. What are a few good arguments to show that the Bible manuscripts were copied reliably?

4. What are the two main Old Testament tests for determining true teaching and true predictive prophecy?

---

2   C.H. Mackintosh, *Notes on the Pentateuch* (Neptune: Loizeaux Brothers, 1972), 215.

5. How might you explain to someone the implications of biblical prophecy as it relates to proof of the divine inspiration of the Bible?

6. What are some of the references in the Bible telling us to check all teaching with Scripture?

7. What is meant by the literal approach to interpreting the Bible?

QUESTIONS PEOPLE ASK

■ *What about all the errors and contradictions in the Bible?*

Rather than errors or contradictions, it might be more accurate to say that there are some *biblical difficulties*. This is not to dodge the issue but to show that many of the so-called errors can be logically and fairly explained. Many times false assumptions are made that lead people to incorrect conclusions. For example, the Bible is not in error simply because an alternate description of an event is told by several authors. This is what takes place in the four gospel accounts of Jesus' life. Unless these accounts specifically contradict one another, there is no error. The accounts merely complement each other. We must be fair-minded and give the authors the benefit of the doubt.

There are apparent contradictions and apparent errors. However, when studied more closely, satisfactory answers can be found. There are many good reference books available that clearly and expertly deal with the problems of biblical difficulties. One such book is by Norman Geisler and Thomas Howe, *When Critics Ask*, Victor Books, 1992. This book has a lengthy introduction that lists seventeen common mistakes people make in dealing with biblical difficulties. This is followed by examples from both the Old and New Testaments.

■ *How was the Bible compiled?*

The compilation of the Bible concerns the issue of canon. That is, the measuring rod (canon) by which some writings were declared to be on par with Scripture and other writings were rejected.

The most basic point that must be realized is that the Bible was written, compiled, and preserved exclusively in the community of the people of Israel. God's plan was to raise up (create) a people for himself. Through Abraham, Isaac, and Jacob, God created a nation of people he could call his own. Scripture was given to Israel. God chose to reveal himself to the world through the people of Israel. They were the caretakers of God's holy word and the revelation of God to the rest of the world. The Apostle Paul made reference to Israel regarding this point:

Theirs is the adoption as sons; theirs the divine glory, the covenants, the receiving of the law, the temple worship and the promises. Theirs are the patriarchs, and from them is traced the human ancestry of Christ (Romans 9:4–5).

Another factor to consider regarding the canon of Scripture is that the writings had to be from a recognized prophet of God. This has often been called the "prophetic principle." Only the prophets were given the authorization to say, "This is what the LORD says."

There is also the task of comparing what was written with what has been written and accepted previously. There could be no contradiction or error regarding what was previously revealed as truth about God (see Deuteronomy 13:1–4).

The Bible wasn't compiled and selected by an anonymous committee, or in a random, haphazard way. Israel was uniquely called to be the shepherds of God's word under the direction of the Holy Spirit.

The New Testament was compiled under the watchful eye of the believing community using the same principles of canon used for the Old Testament.

■ *Hasn't modern science disproved the Bible?*

History is full of horror stories of the clash between science and the Bible. Galileo, himself a devout believer, tried to steer the controversy in his day toward common sense. This is a quote that is associated with him: "The Bible tells us how to go to heaven, not how the heavens go." Many have been led into error by trying to force the Bible to speak to areas for which it was not intended.

The word "science" means "knowledge." To give value to a word making it an entity in and of itself is a mistake. Science is merely what we know. Many people would like to make a dichotomy between what we know and what is commonly called faith. To them, it is as if faith and knowledge cannot mix. True biblical faith is backed by knowledge. To believe otherwise would force us to believe that there is no faith in the realm of science and no science (knowledge) in the realm of faith.

There will always be some mysteries in the Bible, just as there will always be some mysteries in modern science. Many things in the sciences are taken by faith, but usually not without good evidence. The same is true with things pertaining to the Bible. Many things that have been previously unexplainable in both science and the Bible now have acceptable explanations.

Chapter Three

JESUS CHRIST

KEY POINTS

- What the Bible says about the deity of Christ
- What the Bible says about the humanity of Christ
- God's plan for humanity revolves around Christ

> "You can shut him up for a fool, you can spit at him and kill him as a demon; or you can fall at his feet and call him Lord and God. But let us not come up with any patronizing nonsense about his being called a great human teacher. He has not left that open to us. He did not intend to."
>
> —C. S. Lewis in *Mere Christianity*

C. S. Lewis, the great Oxford scholar, was determined to set the record straight: the identity of Jesus Christ is *the* crucial issue. There is no Christianity without a *divine* Christ. Furthermore, the biblical depiction of Jesus clearly leaves no other description of him possible except God in the flesh (John 1:14). This is an essential point that must be understood. We can settle for nothing less. The following seven sections will tell the story of Jesus Christ.

Section One

JESUS CLAIMED TO BE GOD

Read this account of a conversation Jesus had with his disciples:

When Jesus came to the region of Caesarea Philippi, he asked his disciples, "Who do people say the Son of Man is?"

They replied, "Some say John the Baptist; others say Elijah; and still others, Jeremiah or one of the prophets."

"But what about you?" he asked. "Who do you say that I am?"

Simon Peter answered, "You are the Christ, the Son of the living God."

Jesus replied, "Blessed are you, Simon son of Jonah, for this was not revealed to you by man, but by my Father in heaven" (Matthew 16:13–17).

This was an important issue for Jesus: "Who do people say that I am?" He was not about to let his true identity be a thing of rumor. His true identity had to clearly be known.

Some people would like to discount Jesus' own emphasis on his identity. They would like to make Jesus out to be a mere man. Perhaps this would allow them to shelve Jesus along with all the other religious leaders in the world. Jesus did not leave that as an option. Notice that Jesus did not object to Peter's bold proclamation as to his true identity. No one in their right mind would allow for such a description of themselves unless it was true. Also, it could *only* be true of one person. Jesus was (and is) that person.

Matthew 16:13–17 attributes three titles to Jesus.

1. The Christ

In Old Testament history when a king was chosen he was anointed with oil. It was a ceremony marking him as the one who would govern for God in the power of the Holy Spirit. For example, Samuel the prophet was told to go and anoint David as king. *"So Samuel took the horn of oil and anointed him in the presence of his brothers, and from that day on the Spirit of the LORD came upon David in power"* (1 Samuel 16:13). The anointing was a symbol of God's power working through the one who was so anointed.

Israel was promised that eventually *the* Anointed One would be coming. He would have unusual power and *also* have the attributes of God. It was promised that he would bring deliverance and salvation not only to the Jewish nation, but also to the whole world. This was the "Messiah" (the Hebrew term), the "Christ" (the Greek term). Both terms mean the Anointed One.

Jesus wanted to let the religious leaders know that the Christ would not be a mere human being, but much more:

While the Pharisees were gathered together, Jesus asked them, "What do you think about the Christ? Whose son is he?"
"The son of David," they replied.
He said to them, "How is it then that David, speaking by the Spirit, calls him 'Lord'? For he says, 'The Lord said to my Lord:
"Sit at my right hand
until I put your enemies
under your feet."'
If then David calls him 'Lord,' how can he be his own son?" No one *could say a word in reply, and from that day on no one dared to ask him any more questions* (Matthew 22:41–46).

The very clear implication was that the Christ was not merely human, but divine. The religious leaders could not answer Jesus.

They found his point very disturbing. The religious leaders did not want to openly admit that Jesus was the Christ. The man standing in front of them did not match their preconceived ideas as to whom the Christ (The Anointed One) should be. Many people also struggle today with issues regarding the true identity of Christ. Jesus is often considered a mere human being whose calling was to live a life as an example for others to follow. It should be obvious by the quote from Matthew 22 that Jesus was trying to show that he was much more than human.

2. The Son of Man

When Jesus was on trial, the religious leaders questioned him:

The high priest said to him, "I charge you under oath by the living God: Tell us if you are the Christ, the son of God."
"Yes, it is as you say," Jesus replied. "But I say to all of you: In the future you will see the Son of Man sitting at the right hand of the Mighty One and coming on the clouds of heaven" (Matthew 26:63-63).

In the eyes of the religious leaders Jesus was, without question, claiming to be God. This was the reason they were seeking his death: *". . . because you, a mere man, claim to be God"* (John 10:33). They were accusing Jesus of blasphemy, which was punishable by death.

Jesus quoted from Daniel 7 and attributed to himself the title "Son of Man." Daniel foretold that the Son of Man would come as a divine being. Read the following and notice the similarities in Jesus' answer. Also notice that the various descriptions of the Son of Man could only be attributed to a divine being and certainly not to any created being:

In my vision at night I looked, and there before me was one like a son of man, coming with the clouds of heaven. He approached the Ancient of Days and was led into his presence. He was given authority, glory and sovereign power; all peoples, nations and men of every language worshipped him. His dominion is an everlasting dominion that will not pass away, and his kingdom is one that will never be destroyed (Daniel 7:13–14).

This "Son of Man" was given all authority, glory, and sovereign power. He was also worshipped by all people and had a kingdom that would never end. Jesus rightfully took this title, "Son of Man," for himself which had definite, explicit and direct reference to a divine being as foretold by the prophet Daniel.

3. The Son of God

The Koran states, "Far be it from His glory that God should have a son" (Sura 4:169). The teaching in the Koran appears to take exception to the biblical reference to "son of God." This is a misunderstanding that came from placing the usual physical and biological connotations on the word "son" as it related to Jesus. The title, Son of God, does not at all refer to any procreation on God's part. Instead, it refers to essence, sameness, and being of the same order. It speaks of close relationship.

There are many examples in the Bible where the term is used in this manner without the thought of procreation. The prophets who belonged to the larger group of prophets were called the "sons of the prophets" (1 Kings 20:35). Jesus pronounced woes upon the religious leaders and said that they were like their *father*, the devil, because they were just like him (John 8:41–44). Obviously, they were not procreated by the devil, but were being just like him, that is, "sons" of the devil. James and John were called "Sons of Thunder" (Mark 3:17) because it was a good description of their temperaments. In a similar way, Barnabas was called "Son of Encouragement" (Acts 4:36) because it was an accurate description of his character. None of these uses of "son" had to do with the biological sense of the word.

In the same way, Son of God is an accurate description of Jesus. *"… he was even calling God his own Father making himself equal with God"* (John 5:18). As we read earlier in Matthew 26:63, Jesus was questioned about his identity and was asked if he was the Son of God. Jesus gave an affirmative answer.

Having the correct and accurate portrait of Jesus Christ is an essential part of Christianity. There can be no true and powerful Christianity without a proper view of Jesus. The three titles: Christ, Son of Man, and Son of God, are part of the "Name" of Jesus that reveal his character and nature.

Beyond the three titles that have been mentioned, we must also note that all throughout the gospel accounts, Jesus spoke and acted in ways that only God could speak or act. He spoke of *his* angels (Matthew 13:41); he forgave sins (Mark 2:5); he spoke of judging the world (Matthew 25:31–46); he claimed to be Lord of the Sabbath (Mark 2:27,28); he claimed to be one with the Father (John 14:7–9); he claimed preexistence (John 8:58); he had power over life and death (John 11:25); he received worship (John 20:28); and let's not forget his authority over nature as displayed by his miracles.

Jesus clearly and deliberately presented himself to the world as God in the flesh. His claims were evident in the three titles he took upon himself and by his words and by his actions.

ALIAS ALERT

There are many skeptics, even some who call themselves Christians, who say that Jesus was given assumed names and an assumed identity. They say that he never claimed to be anything other than a mere human teacher. These skeptics state that Jesus' claims to deity were myths that were added later by some of his well-meaning followers. This is an ALERT to make you aware of these kinds of challenges. A quick review of the seven section headings in this chapter will show that this is a challenge that can be easily met by a careful and systematic presentation of the facts as recorded in Scripture.

Section Two

JESUS POSSESSES THE TITLES & ATTRIBUTES OF GOD

The following chart depicts ten proofs of the deity of Christ. This chart is merely a convenient way to show that the deity of Christ is not a minor issue. It also shows that it is not an isolated topic relegated solely to the New Testament, but that the deity of Christ is a teaching of the whole Bible. I have used abbreviations for the books of the Bible in some instances to save space. There are many other Scripture verses that could be cited:

		GOD	**JESUS**
1. ATTRIBUTES OF GOD	Holy	Lev 11:45	1 Jn 3:5
	Eternal	Ps 93:2	Heb 13:8
	All-knowing	Jer 17:9,10	Jn 2:25
	All-present	Ps 139:7–12	Mt 28:20
2. TITLES OF GOD	Creator	Isaiah 40:28	Jn 1:8
	Savior	Isaiah 45:22	Jn 4:42
	I AM	Ex 3:14	Jn 8:58
	Lord	Isaiah 45:33	Rom 10:9
	God	Gen 1:1	Heb 1:8
3. JESUS' OWN CLAIMS	Mark 14:61–64		
	John 17:5		
	Revelation 1:8; 22:13		
	John 8:58		
4. CLAIMS OF OTHERS	John 20:28		
	Colossians 2:9		
	John 1:1		
	Matthew 16:15,16		
5. MIRACLES	Luke 7:22		
	Mark 4:35–41		
	Matthew 14:15–21		
	John 11:1–44		

			GOD	**JESUS**
6.	PROPHECY	Born of a woman	Gen 3:15	Gal 4:4
		Born of a virgin	Is 7:14	Mt 1:21
		Cut off (killed)	Dan 9:24	Jn 19:30
		Seed of Abraham	Gen 12:1–3	Mt 1:1
		Tribe of Judah	Gen 49:10	Lk 3:23
		House of David	2 Sam 7:12	Mt 1:1
		Born in Bethlehem	Micah 5:2	Mt 2:1
		Messenger sent	Is 40:3	Mt 3:1,2
		Perform miracles	Is 35:5,6	Mt 9:35
		Cleanse temple	Malachi 3:1	Mt 21:12
		Humiliating death	Psalm 22; Isaiah 53	
		Resurrection	Ps 2:7; 16:10	Acts 2:24–33
		Ascension	Ps 68:8	Acts 1:9
		Right hand of God	Ps 110:1	Heb 1:3
7.	FORGAVE SINS		Mark 2:5	
8.	CREATOR		John 1:1–3	
			Colossians 1:15–17	
9.	RECEIVED WORSHIP		Matthew 14:33	
			John 9:38	
			Hebrews 1:6	
10.	AUTHORITY		Philippians 2:9–11	
			Matthew 28:18	

As shown in this chart, the Bible clearly portrays Jesus having equal status with God. If Jesus was not God, we who worship him, would be guilty of false worship. We all would be idol worshipers and Christianity, as it is known biblically, would have to cease.

Section Three

JESUS FULFILLS OLD TESTAMENT PROPHECIES

The more our study of the Old and New Testament deepens, the more we will grow in our appreciation for the many prophecies concerning Jesus found in the Old Testament. It should strengthen our faith to see them fulfilled in the New Testament. As someone once said, "The New Testament lies hidden in the Old Testament and the Old lies open in the New." Some of the prophecies about Jesus are often called "Messianic" prophecies because they concern the Messiah.

The book of Matthew starts out citing the genealogy of Christ. *"A record of the genealogy of Jesus Christ the son of David, the son of Abraham . . ."* (Matthew 1:1). Those are two immediate prophetic promises fulfilled at the birth of Christ—that the Christ would be a direct descendant of David and Abraham. Upon further reading in Matthew, you will find that he often quotes Old Testament prophecies to enlighten his readers to the importance of their very fulfillment in the life and character of Jesus.

The following are three ways of studying the Old Testament prophecies concerning Christ: (1) Study prophecies that are plainly recorded as being fulfilled in the New Testament. The premise is that if an inspired New Testament writer recognized a prophetic fulfillment, we are on safe ground recognizing the same. A careful reading of the book of Matthew provides a good example of how Old Testament prophecies were used in the New Testament. (2) Make a study of the types and prefigurations of Christ that are evident all throughout the Old Testament. This is often called *typology*. This kind of study helps us see the beautiful and profound correspondence between Old Testament situations and how they can be linked to their ultimate fulfillment in Christ. (3) Study the prophecies that have yet to be fulfilled. These would have to do with the second coming of Christ and the events surrounding his return.

Historically Fulfilled in the New Testament

The life of Jesus as depicted in the four gospel accounts was a direct fulfillment of Old Testament prophecy. For example, it is known that there were more than two dozen prophecies fulfilled in the events involving Jesus' arrest and crucifixion—all in a single day. A few of them are as follows:

Betrayed by a friend	Psalm 42:9	Matthew 26:49–50
Sold for 30 pieces of silver	Zechariah 11:12	Matthew 26:15–16
Forsaken by his disciples	Zechariah 13:7	Mark 14:50
Silent before his accusers	Isaiah 53:7	Matthew 27:12–19
Wounded and bruised	Isaiah 53:5	Matthew 27:26
Beaten and spit upon	Isaiah 50:6	Matthew 26:67
Mocked	Psalm 22:7,8	Matthew 27:31
Hands and feet pierced	Psalm 22:16	Luke 23:33
Crucified with criminals	Isaiah 53:12	Matthew 27:38
Hated him without cause	Psalm 69:4	John 15:25
Gambled for his clothes	Psalm 22:18	John 19:23–24
No bones broken	Psalm 34:20	John 19:33
Pierced in his side	Zechariah 12:10	John 19:34
Buried in a rich man's tomb	Isaiah 53:9	Matthew 27:57–60

There are many more prophecies that Jesus fulfilled that were foretold in the Old Testament and recorded as history in the New Testament. There are too many fulfilled prophecies to credit *chance* for having anything to do with their fulfillment. They were done in a historical setting that would not allow for their fulfillment to be attributed to *myths* formed by Christians years later. This is documented history. This is fact. Let this fact fuel your faith.

Typology

A second way of studying the prophetic portrait of Jesus Christ is to look at the types and prefigurations in the Old Testament.

An example is found in the Feasts of the LORD. The children of Israel were in slavery in Egypt. God sent Moses to free them. The final working of God's plan to free the people was that they were to take the blood of the lamb and place it on the doorframes of their houses. When the judgment of God fell on the Egyptians, God would see the blood and *pass over* the houses of the Israelites. God told them that from then on they would celebrate the "Passover," and it would mark the beginning of the new year for them.

We can read in the New Testament that *"Christ our Passover lamb has been sacrificed"* (1 Corinthians 5:7). We can know with full assurance that what took place in history more than 3,000 years ago was an *act* of God and a *message* from God. The sacrifice of Jesus was prefigured in the act of the Passover. The message is that God will now set us free from our slavery to sin through the sacrifice of Christ. His blood was not placed on the doorframes of houses but was poured out on the cross. There are many such prophetic portraits of Christ in the Old Testament. The Passover lamb is just one of them. They occurred to give us faith and encouragement and to show the power of God as he worked his plan in history. Here is a brief list that can make for a lifetime of profitable study:

- Adam and Christ — Romans 5:14
- The manna in the wilderness — John 6:32–35
- The rock in the wilderness — 1 Corinthians 10:4
- The bronze serpent — John 3:14–15
- The tabernacle and the sacrificial system — (a careful study of these last two
- The 7 feasts of the LORD — categories will show Jesus clearly portrayed)

Hopefully, this list will stimulate your curiosity to study further this fascinating gold mine of truth that is neatly tucked away in the Bible waiting for any seeker to find.

Prophecies Yet to Be Fulfilled

There is a monument in a park adjacent to the United Nations building in New York City called "The Isaiah Wall" with this inscription: *"They will beat their swords into plowshares and their spears into pruning hooks. Nation will not take up sword against nation nor will they train for war anymore"* (Isaiah 2:4). This verse describes just what the world needs. One thing is missing, however. The prophecy will not come about except by the coming of the Messiah to earth. The second coming of Christ, the Messiah, is yet in the future.

The beginning of this verse was omitted which reads, *"He will judge between the nations and will settle disputes for any peoples.* [Then] *they will beat their swords into plowshares . . ."* There will be no peace without the Prince of Peace. The "he" that was left out of the quote on The Isaiah Wall was referring to the Messiah, Jesus Christ.

There are many promises that are yet to be fulfilled that involve the Messiah and worldwide peace. There are a multitude of these end-times prophecies. There is the promise of hope that is alive in many people as they look forward to Christ's return.

A study of future promises like these point to Jesus himself. Below is a partial list:

- Genesis 12:1–3   The whole world will be blessed through the son of Abraham.
- Psalm 2   The Son will be given the earth as an inheritance and he will rule.
- Isaiah 11:1–9   The wolf will live with the lamb and everyone will know the LORD.
- Jeremiah 23:5   There will be justice over the whole earth.
- Daniel 7:13–14   The Son of Man will come with glory to rule the earth.
- Zechariah 14:9   The LORD will be king over the whole earth.
- Revelation 19   The second coming of Christ.

Section Four

THE DEITY OF CHRIST IN THE NEW TESTAMENT

Since the deity of Christ is such an essential issue, it would be good to have a few Scriptures for quick reference. The following five are all found in first chapters of various books of the New Testament:

John 1:1–2

In the beginning was the Word, and the Word was with God and the Word was God. He was with God in the beginning.

Colossians 1:15–17

He is the image of the invisible God, the firstborn over all creation. For by him all things were created: things in heaven and on earth, visible and invisible, whether thrones or powers or rulers or authorities; all things were created by him and for him. He is before all things, and in him all things hold together.

Hebrews 1:3; 8

The Son is the radiance of God's glory and the exact representation of his being, sustaining all things by his powerful word. After he had provided purification for sins, he sat down at the right hand of the Majesty in heaven. (8) But about the Son he says, "Your throne, O God, will last forever, and righteousness will be the scepter of your kingdom."

2 Peter 1:1

Simon Peter, a servant and apostle of Jesus Christ, to those who through the righteous-ness of our God and Savior Jesus Christ have received a faith as precious as ours.

Revelation 1:8

"I am the Alpha and the Omega," says the Lord God, "who is, and who was, and who is to come, the Almighty." (Jesus applied this title to himself in Revelation 22:13)

These small portions of Scripture are sometimes called *proof texts*. These proof texts provide a fast way to support the deity of Christ. However, it is important to remember that the whole teaching of Scripture points to the deity of Christ.

TIME OUT

Take the time to memorize where these proof texts can be found. This will help you as you encounter doubts or confusion about Jesus. It may sound like an elementary exercise, but take the time to practice locating each of these passages in your Bible. As you locate each one, read the passage carefully before moving on to the next one. Do this for a few days to help lock-in the important teaching regarding the identity of Christ.

It is important to be able to quickly locate clear references to the deity of Christ. By training yourself to know where these verses are located, you will be able to use them when sharing the gospel with someone, and your faith will be encouraged as well. There are five quick references:

John 1—Colossians 1—Hebrews 1—2 Peter 1—Revelation 1

Section Five

JESUS ROSE FROM THE DEAD

Without the resurrection of Christ, we have no Christianity. Read the words of the Apostle Paul:

If Christ has not been raised, our preaching is useless and so is your faith. More than that, we are then found to be false witnesses about God, for we have testified about God that he raised Christ from the dead. But he did not raise him if in fact the dead are not raised. For if the dead are not raised, then Christ has not been raised either. And if Christ has not been raised, your faith is futile; you are still dead in your sins. Then those also who have fallen asleep in Christ are lost. If only for this life we have hope in Christ we are to be pitied more than all men (1 Corinthians 15:14–19).

The fact of the resurrection of Christ is an essential truth and cornerstone of the Christian faith. Without the resurrection, there is no Christianity. Everything about the truth and power of our faith in Christ hinges on the fact that Christ did indeed rise from the dead.

Jesus said he would rise again. He said this after he had cleansed the temple in Jerusalem. The religious rulers were upset with him and demanded to know by what authority he could be so bold to do such a thing:

Jesus answered them, "Destroy this temple, and I will raise it again in three days."

The Jews replied, "It has taken forty-six years to build this temple, and you are going to raise it in three days?" But the temple he had spoken of was his body. After he was raised from the dead, his disciples recalled what he had said. Then they believed the Scripture and the words that Jesus had spoken (John 2:19–22).

First of all, who could say such a thing? No one else in the history of mankind has ever dared to make such a claim. All we would have to do is check their graves, which are all occupied. A check on Jesus' grave will show that it is empty. Moreover, the reality of the resurrection of Christ also proved his authority to cleanse the temple—something no one but God could do.

Paul said that Jesus *". . . was declared to be the Son of God by his resurrection from the dead"* (Romans 1:4). Peter said that *". . . it was impossible for death to keep its hold on him"* (Acts 2:24). Peter went on to quote from Psalm 16 where it was prophesied that the Holy One would not be abandoned to the grave nor would he see decay.

The resurrection of Christ was not the grand finale. He also ascended to the right hand of the throne of God. No one but a divine being could do such a thing. The resurrection is the cornerstone of the Christian faith. The resurrection is *the* historic proof of the deity of Christ.

Section Six

THE MYSTERY OF HIS HUMAN LIMITATIONS

Jesus said, *". . . the Father is greater than I"* (John 14:28). How can the claims that Jesus Christ is equal to God be reconciled with what seems to be evidence to the contrary? It may seem difficult to understand the human limitations of Jesus and his claims of deity until we look deeper into what the Bible says about Jesus.

The Bible very plainly states that Jesus is indeed equal with God in nature and in essence. Both are uncreated, eternal, self-existent beings without beginning or end. The best way to reconcile the humanity of Jesus with his divinity is to realize the fact that Jesus took on an *additional* nature—a human nature. *"The word became flesh and dwelt among us . . ."* (John 1:14). The answer to the mystery of the human limitations of Jesus can be found in Philippians chapter two:

Your attitude should be the same as that of Christ Jesus: Who, being in very nature God,   did not consider equality with God something to be grasped, but made himself nothing, taking the very nature of a servant, being made in human likeness. And being found in appearance as a man, he humbled himself and became obedient to death—even death on a cross! Therefore God exalted him to the highest place and gave him the name that is above every name, that at the name of Jesus every knee should bow, in heaven and on earth and under the earth, and every tongue confess that Jesus Christ is Lord, to the glory of God the Father (Philippians 2:5–11).

A very careful reading of this passage shows that Jesus was declared to be *"in very nature God."* Then we are told that, despite his divine nature, he was willing to let go of his divine rights as God. In doing this, he did not *"grasp his equality with God"* — that is, he was willing to let go of his rights as God. Notice he did not let go of his *nature* as God. He took on an *additional* nature—a human nature. In so doing he submitted himself to the limitations common to all humanity (yet without sin).

Jesus went even further than this in his humiliation: *"He made himself nothing, taking the very nature of a servant."* He went still lower: *"He humbled himself and became obedient to death—even death on a cross."*

It is important to recognize that the context of this passage is about humility. If Jesus, being in very nature God (and of equal standing) could humble himself, then we (being of equal standing with each other) should follow his example of humility in our human relationships. If Jesus was only a mere human, then the impact of his willingness to humble himself would not be as dramatic. However, the fact that Jesus is equal to God only makes his humility stand out all the more.

The divine nature of Christ is clearly proclaimed by Paul in the passage in Philippians 2 which ends with Jesus being exalted to the highest place — the place only God can fill. Paul quoted Isaiah 45:23 in the Philippians passage. I will cite verse 22 along with Isaiah 45:23 to set verse 23 in context:

Turn to me and be saved, all you ends of the earth;
For I am God, and there is no other.
By myself I have sworn,
My mouth has uttered in all integrity
A word that will not be revoked:
Before me every knee will bow;
By me every tongue will swear (Isaiah 45:22–23).

In the Philippian passage, we see Jesus as the one before whom the whole world will bow. In the Isaiah passage, we see God receiving the same adulation, thereby making them equals. The mystery of Jesus' human limitations is answered by the fact that his deity was veiled in human flesh. This would make it appear to some that Jesus might have been less than he was. However, he was only living out the incarnation as a real man until such time as he would rise from the dead and ascend to heaven from where he existed and now exists in eternity with God the Father. Jesus knew he would return to the Father and his glory would again be unveiled:

"Father, glorify me in your presence with the glory I had with you before the world began" (John 17:5).

Section Seven

THE SECOND COMING OF CHRIST

Jesus said, *"And if I go and prepare a place for you, I will come back and take you to be with me that you also may be where I am"* (John 14:3). The teaching of the second coming of Christ is throughout the New Testament. As the disciples witnessed the ascension of the Lord into the clouds, they were told, *"Men of Galilee, why do you stand here looking into the sky? This same Jesus, who has been taken from you into heaven, will come back in the same way you have seen him go into heaven"* (Acts 1:11).

The amazing event of the second coming will be the final, culminating act of God upon this world. It will be the end of the age. It will be the end of life on earth as we know it. Without getting into the many theories concerning the timing of this great event, we can be sure that the second coming of Christ will be God's final curtain on human history. As C. S. Lewis once said, "When the author walks on stage, the play is over." As the book of Revelation says: *"The kingdom of the world has become the kingdom of our Lord and of his Christ, and he will reign for ever and ever"* (Revelation 11:15).

CONCLUSION

Recall the discussion when Peter gave his great confession as to the identity of Jesus as the Christ, the Son of the Living God? (see section one) Jesus said to Peter that he was "blessed" (Matthew 16:17). To be blessed means to be highly favored of God. It was proof that God was working in Peter's life; otherwise, he could not have made such a confession.

If you can make the same confession as Peter, then you too are "blessed" just like Peter. If you can make the same confession as Peter then place your name in the blank. Let this truth sink into your heart.

"Blessed are you, _____, for this was not revealed to you by man, but by my Father in heaven" (Matthew 16:17).

If you can call on the name of Christ as your Lord and Savior, and you know him as the Son of the Living God, you are indeed blessed of God. It is proof that God is at work in your life.

TIME OUT

Go over the seven categories that give a description of the nature of Jesus Christ. The more you become aware of these categories that mark the nature and being of Christ, the more your faith will increase. Be able to recall these seven highlights that refer to the person and work of Christ.

1. Jesus claimed to be God.
2. Jesus possesses the titles and attributes of God.
3. Jesus fulfills Old Testament prophecies.
4. The deity of Christ is clearly taught in the New Testament.
5. Jesus rose from the dead.
6. Jesus took on an additional nature in becoming human.
7. Jesus will return.

The fact of the true identity of Jesus Christ is central to the Christian faith. That's why we are called "Christians," and that is why we are right to worship Christ. In our first chapter we discovered how important the Bible was in our understanding of the nature of our faith. In this chapter we have discovered how important our understanding of the nature of Christ is to our faith. A weak view of the Bible will give us a weak view of Christ. A weak view of Christ will give us a weak view of our salvation. It is our salvation that we will study in the next chapter.

STUDY QUESTIONS

1. Can you explain the meaning behind these titles: Christ, Son of God and Son of Man?

2. Can you list three or four attributes and/or prerogatives of God that can also be attributed to Jesus?

3. How many Old Testament prophecies can you name that have found their fulfillment in Christ?

4. How would you explain what is meant by *typology* and give an example as it relates to Jesus Christ?

5. Can you list three proof texts regarding the deity of Christ?

6. What New Testament passage best explains the mystery of the human limitations of Christ?

QUESTIONS PEOPLE ASK

■ *Doesn't the fact that Jesus is called the "firstborn" mean that he is less than God?*

In Old Testament times the firstborn male was given the title of "firstborn." This meant that he would have the first place position in the inheritance rights that were passed down from the patriarch of the family. The person designated firstborn would also receive a double inheritance as a way to honor his position as the next patriarch (ruler) of the family.

It makes for an interesting study in the lives of Abraham and Isaac to discover that neither of their firstborn sons received the title of firstborn. Ishmael was born first, yet the title went to Isaac who was born second. Jacob was born after Esau, yet Jacob received the title. David was born the eighth son to Jesse, yet he was given the title of firstborn in a prophetic sense because the Messiah, the son of David, would rule forever. Please read Psalm 89:27 and context.

This should give us a clue that birth order does not necessarily determine who will be given the title firstborn. This is because it is not as much about birth as it is about who will rule. In the case of Jesus, he was given the title to show that he has absolute sovereignty. Therefore, when Colossians 1:15 states that Jesus is *"the firstborn over all creation"* it means that he is Lord of creation.

We must remember that Jesus did not have to be born in order to exist. The Bible states the fact that Jesus has no beginning and no end. He is eternal with the Father. He became God incarnate (in the flesh) as he entered creation through the virgin birth. Jesus Christ rules as "the firstborn over all creation."

■ *Why did the Jews reject and kill Jesus?*

The overwhelming majority of believers in the beginning of the church were Jews. Jesus was a Jew. All of his disciples were Jews. Almost all of the New Testament writers were Jews. Christianity is Jewish. The Jewish nature of Christianity is often overlooked. It is not completely accurate to say that the Jews rejected Jesus because of the fact that many, many Jews *did* receive Jesus as their Savior. It is interesting that, at first, the *Jewish* believers had trouble accepting the non-Jews who placed their faith in Christ (see Acts 15). This helps to show just how Jewish Christianity was at its beginning stages.

Once this is understood, we can say the Jews did "officially" reject Jesus. The religious leadership in power at the time rejected him. So, in that limited sense, it can be said that the Jews rejected Jesus. However, we must be careful not to cast aspersions on the Jews who rejected Jesus, any more than we do on people choosing to reject Jesus today.

Also, the Jews did not kill Jesus. The Romans did. Furthermore, it was all in God's plan. Peter (a Jew) was quick to point out that Jesus was handed over to the crowds to be killed *"by God's set purpose and foreknowledge"* (Acts 2:23). Jesus himself said, *"No one takes it* [my life] *from me, but I lay it down of my own accord"* (John 10:18).

This question of the Jews needs to be answered because it can be used as a smoke screen to avoid the inherent responsibility carried by *all* of humanity regarding the death of Jesus Christ. To foist blame on any one people group is to miss the central issue of the gospel itself. Jesus said, *"I have come not to be served, but to serve, and to give my life as a ransom for many"* (Mark 10:45, paraphrased). It is very certain to me that no one kneeling at a church altar for the first time to receive salvation from sin would ever imagine to cast blame on anyone for killing Jesus. Instead the thought would be, "Thank you, Jesus, for dying on the cross for me."

■ *Do we know when Jesus will return?*

Here's the short answer: no. Please read the following long answer, which is necessary so that the short answer can be understood:

Jesus spoke of his return. *"No one knows about that day or hour, not even the angels in heaven, nor the Son, but only the Father"* (Matthew 24:36).

Three more times in Matthew 24, and a fifth time in Matthew 25:13, Jesus explicitly stated that no one knows the day of his return. It is safe to say Jesus was adamant that the time of his return was to be a sovereign mystery. *Five times*, within the distance of about twenty-five verses, we are told that no one knows the day of the return of Christ. Only God knows.

We can read in Acts, chapter one, that after Jesus rose from the dead he appeared to his disciples for a period of forty days and taught them many things about the kingdom of God. Those must have been very rich teaching sessions about all kinds of topics. It is instructive that we are not told what Jesus taught except for one or two little morsels. Here's one: *"Lord, are you at this time going to restore the kingdom to Israel?" Jesus said to them, "It is not for you to know the times or dates the Father has set by his own authority"* (Acts 1:6–7).

Let's review. Five times, in a short section in Matthew, Jesus stated that no one knows when the second coming of Christ will be: not the angels in heaven and not even the Son. Then, in Acts 1:7, we are told that we are *not* to know. Despite this very explicit and clear teaching from the Second Person of the Trinity, there are those who still persist in thinking that they know more than God Incarnate.

Some people justify their right to set a date for the return of Christ by citing a verse from the prophet Amos. *Surely the Sovereign LORD does nothing without revealing his plan to his servants the prophets* (Amos 3:7).

This verse is understood as an absolute prerequisite that God must reveal *all* of his plans to his servants the prophets before he can act. Honest students of the Bible must ask themselves if this is what this verse means. The answer is no.

Amos was employing hyperbole. Hyperbole is the use of exaggeration to make a point. We all use hyperbole at times. For example, a person who is worried about something might say, "There's a ton of weight on my shoulders." No one thinks that there is a literal 2,000 lb. weight on this person. It's hyperbole. It's an exaggeration to make a point. Worry is crushing him. We understand the intended meaning rather than taking the hyperbole literally.

Amos was using hyperbole to make it very clear to those hearing his message that what he was prophesying regarding Israel would be fulfilled without any doubt. Therefore, people had better listen closely to him. Hyperbolic language is used throughout the Bible. To press hyperbole beyond the scope of the common rules of language leads to misunderstanding. Below are three principles that will help us learn to read the Bible properly.

THREE PRINCIPLES TO REMEMBER WHEN READING SCRIPTURE

1. Interpret smaller passages with larger passages

Another way to state this rule is to say that "Scripture interprets Scripture." We compare a small portion of Scripture with larger portions. Ultimately, we must consider all of Scripture in context as we interpret any smaller portion. Therefore, if we are told something very plainly and often, we are not to use a single verse to counter that teaching. We keep the smaller portion in context with the whole. We are very clearly and plainly told by Jesus himself that we are *not* to know the time of his return. To use one verse in Amos to counter a clearer teaching will lead to error.

Take another look at the verse in Amos. Notice the hyperbole. If we don't notice the hyperbole, the verse becomes meaningless. If the Sovereign LORD does nothing without revealing his plan to his servants the prophets, then the Sovereign LORD is no longer sovereign. Of course God has done things without revealing his plans to his prophets. Common sense should tell us that God has done a multitude of things without first consulting his prophets. Plus, we have Jesus himself (speaking from his human nature) that HE doesn't know when he will return, and it can be easily argued that Jesus outranks any other human prophet who ever existed, or ever will exist.

If people were truly interested in what the Sovereign LORD had to say, they would obey him. A careful reading of the accounts in

Matthew 24–25, Acts 1, and other passages about the return of Christ will show that these passages are clearly focused on obedience and discipleship, not on guessing the date of the second coming of Christ.

2. Know the two main tests for a false prophet or a false teacher.

TEST # 1 — False Teaching

If a prophet, or one who foretells by dreams, appears among you and announces to you a miraculous sign or wonder, and if the sign or wonder of which he spoke takes place, and he says, "Let us follow other gods: (gods you have not known) "and let us worship them," you must not listen to the words of that prophet or dreamer. The LORD your God is testing you to find out whether you love him with all your heart and all your soul. It is the LORD your God you must follow, and him you must revere (Deuteronomy 13:1–4).

Events that appear to be miraculous do not supersede Scripture. This is a difficult test because human nature gravitates toward the sensational. But here, we see that God is concerned about teaching. No miracle of any kind must lead a person to accept false teaching. All teaching must be measured by what has been already revealed by God and has become Scripture.

TEST # 2 — False Prophecy

You may say to yourselves, "How can we know when a message has not been spoken by the LORD?" If what a prophet proclaims in the name of the LORD does not take place or come true, that is a message the LORD has not spoken. The prophet has spoken presumptuously. Do not be afraid of him (Deuteronomy 18:21-22).

God demands one hundred percent accuracy on any predictions of future events. The premise should be obvious: God makes no mistakes. At times religious leaders make bold proclamations of future events that do not transpire as predicted. Such failures are properly categorized as false prophecy and we are instructed not to give credibility to these false prophets. This leads to a third principle.

TEST # 3. Personal Responsibility

Personal responsibility comes under the heading of discipleship. Jesus left us with his very famous last words in the book of Matthew: *All authority in heaven and on earth has been given to me. Therefore go and make disciples of all nations, baptizing them in the name of the Father and of the Son and of the Holy Spirit, and teaching them to obey everything I have commanded you. And surely I am with you always, to the very end of the age* (Matthew 28:17–20).

Please notice what Jesus was concerned about at the end of the age. It was not that we would know the time of his coming but that we would be his disciples. A disciple is a learner. Disciples are people who are willing to learn how to obey. Religious leaders are not exempt from the call to learn how to obey. They, too, are called to obey God's Word.

Every believer is personally responsible to know Scripture. It is hard to know how to obey something if you don't know what it is you are to obey. One of the reasons so many false teachers can get away with their errant predictions of the return of Christ is that too many believers are asleep spiritually—the very thing Jesus was warning about when discussing the time of his return.

We must take up the mantle of discipleship. We are called to test all things to determine truth (see 1 Thessalonians 5:17). We are called to be like the Bereans (see Acts 17:11). We are not to believe everything, but test teachings (see 1 John 4:1). This is our personal responsibility.

Chapter Four

SALVATION

KEY POINTS

- Creation was made perfect
- Creation is now fallen
- There is only ONE plan of salvation

Human history is riddled with unspeakable atrocities. Whether nation against nation or person against person, one thing remains the same: evil has entrenched itself deeply within our world. There is no sign of evil disappearing any time soon.

Sitting before our TV sets we are bombarded by an amazing steady stream of indecent acts committed on foreign soil and on our own. The bad news knows no boundaries. Perhaps we become so used to all the newscasters who report in their trained announcer voices that we have lost the ability to be amazed at all. We hear about evil every day and maybe have grown a little numb. Yet, the question of the existence of evil continues to haunt all of us.

Imagine, if by some stroke of magic, the news was reported with a little different slant: "An armed robbery took place today at First National Bank. The robber got away with an undisclosed amount of cash after shooting two bank guards and one teller. They are in serious condition, but are expected to recover from their wounds. An all-points bulletin has gone out to find the person who committed this *sin*. In other news, four youths were apprehended as they committed the *sin* of vandalism at the local elementary school. In international news, the nation of Sardon has *sinned* by invading the territory of Krabitz. I'm sorry to report that many deaths of innocent civilians have resulted because of this *sin*. Now a message from our sponsor."

A newscast such as this will never take place because our secular world will not allow that three-letter word "sin" into the national vocabulary. Does the omission of that word from our collective vocabulary mean that, although we are mystified by the ever-present evil all around us, we have failed to discern the true cause of this evil? As we come to terms with the *biblical* meaning behind that little word *sin*, the mystery of evil will become much less a mystery and much more a sobering reality. As the light begins to shine on the reality of sin, the light will also shine on the solution. We will discover the underlying problem that is behind the calamities that have afflicted humanity ever since history began and we will also learn about the answer.

In this chapter on salvation we will look at the nature of the problem that confronts all of humanity, and we will also look at the remedy. The remedy is contained in what has been called the gospel. Gospel comes from the Old English word, *godspel*, or good-story. The Old English word came from the Greek word *eu* (good) *angel* (message). From this word we get *evangel* and *evangelism*. So, the gospel (good news) is spread via an evangelist: one who proclaims good news. This good news is the best news of all.

AVERSION ALERT

Many people have an aversion to words like *salvation* and *sin*. Words like these bring up negative images in their minds. Some may have mental images of fire and brimstone preachers leaning over pulpits pointing bony fingers at cowering congregations. These words may seem archaic and outdated to our modern ears. This is an ALERT to warn of the danger of using the calendar to determine reality.

Allow yourself to be open to the truth in these words and the value in applying them when they are relevant. A proper biblical understanding will reveal that the words *sin* and *salvation* have an overwhelming value and effect on understanding and improving our civilization today. Therefore, they remain highly relevant in today's world.

Section One

HOW WE GOT HERE

Before we can comprehend the horrendous problem of sin in the world we must first get a clear understanding of how we got into this fix in the first place. We must go to the beginning. We must go the book of beginnings: the Book of Genesis. The first three chapters of Genesis give the complete picture of the human dilemma. Understanding these first three chapters paves the way for the satisfactory and complete answer to the distress that is endured by all humanity.

OVERVIEW OF GENESIS 1–3

Genesis 1: The Creation

"In the beginning God created the heavens and the earth." The emphasis in the first chapter of Genesis is on creation in a general sense. God placed his blessing on creation by pronouncing a divine benediction over each phase, *"and God saw that it was good."* After the sixth day we are given this summary: *"God saw all that he had made and it was very good"* (Genesis 1:31).

There is no doubt that God wanted to stress that his creation was good, very good. Repetition served as the poetic device to capture our attention. It also served notice on anyone who might want to say that creation did not get off to a *good* start. It was, by God's own appraisal, "very good." It was, in fact, Paradise.

Genesis 2: The Probation

The emphasis in chapter two now shifts from creation in general to God's relationship with Adam and Eve specifically. They become the focus in the second chapter. The emphasis is on their capacity for free moral choice. This has often been called their probationary period. It was a time of testing:

And the LORD God commanded the man, "You are free to eat from any tree in the garden; but you must not eat from the tree of the knowledge of good and evil, for when you eat of it you will surely die" (Genesis 2:16–17).

While Adam and Eve were free, they were not independent moral agents. They could enjoy freedom and paradise as long as they remained under the provision and the protection of their Creator. They were free, yet at the same time, accountable. God did not *ask* them not to eat, but he gave them a *command*. Failure to follow God's command would later prove to have drastic, eternal consequences.

Genesis 3: The Fall

The serpent used three lies to tempt Adam and Eve. First, the serpent cast doubt on the veracity of God's word: *"Did God really say?"* Then he moved to the area of God's prescribed consequence for disobedience: *"You will not surely die."* His third and last statement was meant to portray God as having less than honorable motives: *"God knows that when you eat of it your eyes will be opened, and you will be like God, knowing good and evil."*(Genesis 3:1-5). The lies were believed, and Adam and Eve became their own independent moral agents. They found themselves thrust out from under God's protective covering.

Charles Mackintosh spoke of the deception this way:

> Satan had said, "your eyes shall be opened, and you shall be as gods, knowing good and evil"; but he had left out a material part of the truth, namely, that they should know good without the power to do it, and that they should know evil without the power to avoid it. Their very attempt to elevate themselves in the scale

of moral existence involved the loss of true elevation. They became degraded, powerless, Satan-enslaved, conscience-smitten, terrified creatures. "The eyes of them both were opened," no doubt; but, alas! To what a sight!—it was only to discover their own nakedness. [3]

Adam and Eve had to live with the startling discovery that they were not really the free moral agents that they thought they were. They were still accountable to God. There were consequences. They found themselves and all of creation under a curse. The saga of the fall ends with what must have been a terribly sad sight as Adam and Eve were banished and driven out of the Garden of Eden. It was death indeed—spiritual death. Physical death would follow in due time.

An essential part of understanding God's plan of redemption is that we must come to terms with the fact that we are fallen creatures who live in a fallen world. This is the reason we get sick and die. This is the reason why there is crime, war, and national calamities. This is the reason for the pain and suffering we see all around us.

TIME OUT

Now would be a good time to get alone with your Bible and read through the first three chapters of Genesis. It would be good to reread them a few more times as you work through this chapter. So much of what is revealed in the first three chapters of Genesis plays a vital role in God's plan of redemption that makes up the remainder of biblical history.

God's plan of redemption and the power of the Christian message are dependent on a clear understanding of the beginnings of human history that are contained in the first three chapters of Genesis. The importance of these chapters cannot be overstressed. Know these chapters well.

---

3   Charles H. Mackintosh, *Genesis to Deuteronomy* (Neptune: Loizeaux Brothers, 1972), 31.

The first three chapters of Genesis contain many more interesting truths; however, these three elements—creation, probation, and the fall—are vital to a clear understanding of God's beautiful plan of redemption. Let's take a look at God's plan of redemption and how it has been worked out through history.

OVERVIEW OF THE OLD TESTAMENT

The Building of a Nation

The world at large was not interested in a relationship with God as evidenced by the events leading up to the flood and the tower of Babel. God chose to work out his plan of salvation beginning with the calling of one man. That man was Abraham:

The LORD had said to Abram, "Leave your country, your people and your father's household and go to the land I will show you. I will make you into a great nation and I will bless you; I will make your name great, and you will be a blessing. I will bless those who bless you, and whoever curses you I will curse; and all the peoples on earth will be blessed through you" (Genesis 12:1–3).

Rather than giving his attention to the whole world, God would now work through one man. From that one man God built a nation. Through this nation God's plan of redemption would reach the whole world. Through Abraham came Isaac, and through Isaac came Jacob. Jacob had twelve sons who made up the twelve tribes of Jacob. (God later changed Jacob's name to Israel). Out of all the nations on earth, the Messiah would come from the family of Jacob (Israel). This was the reason that, in God's promise to Abraham, the whole world would be blessed through him. The Messiah would be a descendant of Abraham.

The Making of a Covenant

When it came time for God to give the Promised Land to Israel, he established a covenant with them. This was a covenant that would show that they belonged to the one true God in the midst of a world population that served many gods. The Ten Commandments served as a condensation of the laws of the covenant:

And God spoke all these words: "I am the LORD your God, who brought you out of Egypt, out of the land of slavery. You shall have no other gods before me" (Exodus 20:1–3).

God introduced himself in the preamble leading into the Ten Commandments. He made it known that he alone was worthy due to his miraculous intervention in rescuing his people out of Egypt. The first commandment was that they should have no other gods before him. The covenant stipulated that God should have exclusive sovereignty over his people. This relationship is what the covenant jealously guarded.

The Ten Commandments have often been reduced to a mere list of do's and don'ts. Perhaps they were suitable to hang on a wall, but that's about it. Take a close look at each commandment, and you'll see that there was an overwhelming desire by God to protect and provide for the people who belonged to him. He set out clear moral boundaries for how they were to relate to him as well as how the people should behave toward one another. The Ten Commandments were more than just a list. The issue was about the God behind the list. It spoke of relationship. It was God entering into a covenant relationship with people he called his own. When it came time for the people to ratify the covenant, we can read where the people agreed to do everything that God commanded. The covenant was put into action. The LORD would be their God, and they would be his people.

The remainder of the Old Testament is the account of how this covenant was kept (or not kept) by the people. The sad fact was that the people could not live up to the terms of the covenant. The lure of the false gods and false worship of the surrounding world was too strong for them to resist. The people eventually found themselves losing the Promised Land. The strength of the covenant depended on the ability of the people to remain faithful. The people were found wanting. The covenant eventually became useless. It was broken beyond repair. However, God proved his faithfulness. Even in the midst of human failure, God promised a New Covenant.

The Promise of a New Covenant

As time passed, Israel became a divided nation with Israel to the north (ten tribes) and Judah to the south (two tribes). The prophet Jeremiah was witness to the final collapse by the Babylonian invasion in 586 B.C. The northern nation, Israel, had already disappeared more than 100 years earlier at the hands of the Assyrians in 722 B.C. The Promised Land was lost because the people had broken the covenant beyond repair. Read Deuteronomy 28 for insight into the ramifications of either obeying or disobeying the covenant.

God repeatedly warned the people of the inevitability of judgment due to their repeated disobedience. God used the prophet Jeremiah for many of these warnings. In the midst of the cry for judgment, there was also the shout of the promise of redemption and restoration. It would be the promise of a new covenant.

"The time is coming, declares the LORD, "when I will make a new covenant with the house of Israel and with the house of Judah. It will not be like the covenant I made with their forefathers when I took them by the hand to lead them out of Egypt, because they broke my covenant, though I was a husband to them," declares the LORD. "This is the covenant I will make with the house of Israel after that time," declares the LORD. "I will put my law in their minds and write it on their hearts. I will be their God, and they will be my people. No longer will a man teach his neighbor, or a man his brother, saying 'know the LORD,' because they will all know me, from the least of them to the greatest," declares the LORD. "For I will forgive their wickedness and will remember their sins no more" (Jeremiah 31:31–34).

As this passage clearly shows, the God of the Old Testament was a God of love. Many people have the misconception that that God has somehow changed into a kinder, gentler God in the New Testament. Be assured that God does not, and has not, changed. God's plan is secure since before the creation of the world. We will see how God will bring his many promises of redemption to historical fulfillment through Jesus Christ.

This first section has dealt with how we got into this predicament as sinful human beings in a fallen world. We were created in the image of God, and all was good by God's own proclamation. Then sin entered into God's creation and resulted in the fall. We now are fallen beings living in a fallen world. This is where we are. Now, let's look at where we are going.

Section Two

WHERE WE ARE GOING

The way we are going should be the way God wants us to go. If you are a believer then you have made God's way your way. The rest of the unbelieving world is still saying, "No way." We often recoil because there is something within human nature that rebels at the thought of being told what to do. Maybe you resisted for a long time. I know I did. The message of the Bible tells us that we do not measure up to God's standards and we must submit to his way. This rubs most human beings the wrong way. Let's look at the third chapter from the book of John for more insight.

<u>The Example of Nicodemus</u>

Now there was a man of the Pharisees named Nicodemus, a member of the Jewish ruling council. He came to Jesus at night and said, "Rabbi, we know you are a teacher who has come from God. For no one could perform the miraculous signs you are doing if God were not with him."

In reply Jesus declared, "I tell you the truth, no one can see the kingdom of God unless he is born again" (John 3:1–3).

Jesus saw right into the heart of Nicodemus as he deflected Nicodemus' polite greeting and instead addressed his deepest need. Nicodemus was hit broadside by what Jesus had to say about his inability to "see the kingdom of God." If anyone would qualify for kingdom inclusion, Nicodemus would be the one. He would have been voted by his peers as "most likely to succeed."

First, Nicodemus was a Jew. Who better to have access to the kingdom of God? As the apostle Paul said about the Jews:

Theirs is the adoption as sons; theirs the divine glory, the covenant, the receiving of the law, the temple worship and the promises. Theirs are the patriarchs, and from them is traced the human ancestry of Christ (Romans 9:4–5).

Jesus' statement was not at all what Nicodemus expected to hear. Nicodemus saw himself as one who belonged to the kingdom of God from birth. Jesus said otherwise. If this was true of Nicodemus, how much more would this apply to those who were not as privileged?

Second, Nicodemus was a Pharisee. He had attained a level of spiritual authority and holiness that few could ever hope to attain. The people regarded the Pharisees with the highest esteem. Yet, according to Jesus, Nicodemus was still lacking something.

Third, Nicodemus was a member of the Jewish Sanhedrin, the high court and ruling body of Israel at the time. Most people could easily assume that someone with all of this going for him would have a part in the kingdom of God.

Fourth, Nicodemus was a man with a humble heart. He had a good heart. We know this because Jesus opened up to him in a way that he reserved for people who were receptive. We have further evidence because Nicodemus later became a disciple. Nicodemus could be considered, by human standards, a good man and well-liked by all. Nicodemus had every human quality that most people would naturally assume could measure up to God's standards of a good, acceptable man.

We are forced to consider this question: if, of all people, Nicodemus could not measure up, who can? The answer is, no one. Nicodemus was a bit troubled by his conversation with Jesus, but he was willing to listen. Many people, when confronted with their own need of salvation, are not always as willing as Nicodemus to listen. The central issue of salvation is that it must be *God's* way. You must be born again.

Jesus informed Nicodemus that, as a descendent of Adam, he was born spiritually dead. He was born spiritually separated from God. He needed to experience the regeneration that could only come from the Holy Spirit. The Old Covenant could do nothing for him. New birth is exclusively a product of the New Covenant. It comes from placing one's trust in Jesus Christ. There is no other way to be "born again."

One Way

There is only one way to God. It is through God's provision through Christ. *Jesus answered, "I am the way and the truth and the life. No one comes to the Father but by me"* (John 14:6).

Salvation is found in no one else, for there is no other name under heaven given to men by which we must be saved (Acts 4:12).

There are many other Scriptures that can be cited to show that God has only one plan, and Jesus is that plan. In the ancient history of Israel, God had set up an elaborate tabernacle system with many rituals and a special priesthood. There was only *one* tabernacle available and only *one* priesthood. It would not have done anyone any good to set up their own tabernacle and priesthood system when God himself had already set up his prescribed way. Not only would it make no sense, but also it would be in direct disobedience to God's will. In the same way, Jesus is God's only mediator today:

For there is one God and mediator between God and men, the man Christ Jesus, who gave himself as a ransom for all men (1 Timothy 2:5–6).

<u>Selected Scriptures</u>

There are certain Bible passages that lay out the way of salvation. It is important when reading these to realize that the plan of salvation is incorporated in the teaching of the whole Bible that pertains to the New Covenant. However, using specific passages helps us to locate the truth in a succinct manner. For a more complete teaching on salvation, Romans 1—8 gives a powerful explanation of the gospel.

The following passages give a quick glimpse into the way of salvation:

Yet to all who received him, to those who believed in his name, he gave the right to become children of God—children born not of natural descent, nor of human decision or a husband's will, but born of God (John 1:12–13).

"I tell you the truth, whoever hears my word and believes him who sent me has eternal life and will not be condemned; he has crossed over from death to life" (John 5:24).

For all have sinned and fall short of the glory of God, and are justified freely by his grace through the redemption that came by Christ Jesus (Romans 3:23–24).

For the wages of sin is death, but the gift of God is eternal life in Christ Jesus our Lord. (Romans 6:23–24).

For it is by grace you have been saved, through faith—and this not from yourselves, it is the gift of God—not by works, so that no one can boast (Ephesians 2:8–9).

Section Three

WHO WE ARE

This section will explore two issues: (1) assurance of our salvation and (2) growth in our salvation. A study in these areas places the focus on who we are in Christ. We must come to a correct understanding of how God sees us in Christ. This will revolutionize our lives and bring untold blessing. Once our identity in Christ becomes more real to us, we have the opportunity to grow in Christ. Our faith and gratitude will move us to become mature in our faith.

Assurance of Our Salvation

God wants all who belong to him through Jesus Christ to *know* that they belong to him. In other words, we are to know we are saved. It's part of building our relationship with God. We all need to know how *God* sees us in Christ and have a firm foundation on which to base our relationship with him: *"I write these things to you who believe in the name of the Son of God so that you may know that you have eternal life"* (1 John 5:13).

There are two problems that plague anyone who has entered into a relationship with God through the salvation that comes through Jesus Christ.

Problem #1: "I don't feel saved."

The solution to this problem is to ask yourself the question: "Have I trusted in Christ?" If you can answer, "Yes," then you are equipped to take God at his word. Read some of the verses listed earlier and apply them directly to your life now.

God's plan of salvation goes contrary to human nature. We naturally feel that we must somehow *earn* right relationship with God: "I don't measure up. I feel guilt. Therefore, I must do something to make myself pleasing to God." It is hard to accept the gospel of grace. We may never *feel* saved. God would wean us away from dependence on feelings and natural thinking. God's plan is that we all learn what it is to depend on the promises in his word. God's word tells us who we are. Put your faith in God's word, and your feelings will soon follow.

Problem #2: "I still sin."

We may or may not feel saved, but we will *always* sin. This is a hard lesson that must be learned. It should lead to humility and a life-style of repentance:

If we claim to be without sin, we deceive ourselves and the truth is not in us. If we confess our sins, he is faithful and just and will forgive us our sins and purify us from all unrighteousness. If we claim we have not sinned, we make him out to be a liar and his word has no place in our lives (1 John 1:8–10).

John made it clear in his letter that we all sin. What we need to do is confess our sins before God. It becomes a daily way of life for the believer. The key verse wedged between verses eight and ten is verse nine. We must keep short accounts with God by refusing to ignore sin if we have indeed sinned. While our eternal life remains secure in Christ, our communion with God may be damaged by sin. Confession is the way back to open communion with God.

TIME OUT

Write out 1 John 1:9 on a separate piece of paper and memorize it. Confession is agreeing to what God already knows about us. If we know we have sinned, we are invited to confess our sin to God.

As you take the time to memorize and meditate on 1 John 1:9, you will see that God is faithful and just. He is faithful because he will always do what he has promised. He is just because justice was served on the cross on our behalf. He will even go beyond anything we could hope for. He will cleanse us from *all* unrighteousness. Put this promise to work in your life.

Assurance of salvation may take some time and many struggle with their assurance for years. Assurance of our salvation is the foundation for future growth. Knowing who we are in Christ will help us rest assured in that salvation.

Growth In Our Salvation

To grow in our salvation means to have our relationship with God develop over time. Our relationship with God should become more and more fruitful and satisfying. This is why we can say that salvation is so much more than just having our sins forgiven. We have the never-ending joy of growing and deepening our relationship with God:

Grow in the grace and knowledge of our Lord and Savior Jesus Christ (2 Peter 3:18).

Like newborn babies, crave pure spiritual milk, so that by it you may grow up in your salvation. (1 Peter 2:2).

"This is to my Father's glory that you bear much fruit, showing yourselves to be my disciples" (John 15:8).

Growth and fruitfulness are a part of our salvation. One of the functions of the church is to help believers grow toward maturity. The function of the church will be covered in the next chapter.

CONCLUSION

Coming to terms with God's plan of salvation is not as easy as it might seem at first. It is a free gift, yet very costly. It cost God his Son. It cost Jesus more than we can ever understand. Yes, God's plan of salvation is free. On one hand it is simple, yet it can also be deeper than anyone will ever be able to understand.

There is a spiritual battle going on for the souls of people. Truth is hard to come by and accepting God's truth is even harder. Charles Mackintosh presented the problem of this spiritual resistance.

> [There is] the remarkable contrast between the testimony set up in Eden and that which is set up now. Then, while all around was *life*, God spoke of *death;* now, on the contrary, when all around is death, God speaks of life: then, the word was, "in the day thou eatest thou shalt die"; now, the word is, "believe and *live*." And, as in Eden the enemy sought to make void God's testimony as to the result of eating the fruit, so now he seeks to make void God's testimony as the result of believing the gospel. God had said, "In the day that you eatest thereof thou shalt surely *die*"; but the serpent said, "ye shall not surely *die*." And now, when God's word plainly declares that "he that believeth on the Son *hath* everlasting *life*" (John 3:36), the same serpent seeks to persuade people that they have *not* everlasting *life*. [4]

If you can say without a doubt that you are "saved," then you have participated in one of the greatest miracles of all time. God created the universe at his command. The universe did not have a choice in the matter, nor was it held responsible. He could command a universe into existence, but he will not command rebels to turn to him against their will. God has given all people the freedom of choice to say "no" to him. The fact that God offers the world a way of salvation through Jesus Christ is a reality that should humble all people.

STUDY QUESTIONS

1.   What are the central themes of the first three chapters of Genesis?

---

4 Mackintosh, ibid. 27–28.

2. What are the benefits of Abraham's call in Genesis 12:1–3?

3. How many differences can you name between the Old Covenant and the New?

4. What does it mean to be born again?

5. Can you name four Scriptures that claim Jesus as the only way to salvation?

6. Can you recite 1 John 1:9 from memory?

7. What would you say to a Christian who didn't feel saved?

QUESTIONS PEOPLE ASK

■ *If God knew that Adam and Eve would sin, why didn't he create them with the ability not to sin?*

First of all, proposing a "what if?" scenario is useless because it cannot change reality. Gravity causes things to fall toward the earth, and sometimes people get hurt. Wishing it were somehow different will not change reality. The fact that we live in a fallen world is the reality we all must live with.

God created human beings with a free will. Love demands that free will be exercised. Robots cannot love. We choose to love. What kind of love would it be if people had to be coerced against their will? God gave human beings freedom to choose him or to reject him. Adam and Eve rejected God, and the results were catastrophic. The good news is that now, through Jesus Christ, the effects of the Fall can be reversed. *"God so loved the world that he gave his one and only Son, that whoever believes in him shall not perish, but have eternal life"* (John 3:16). Anyone can make the choice today and be one of the "whoevers" of John 3:16. All they have to do is believe in Christ.

■ *Isn't it being narrow-minded to say that Jesus is the only way to salvation?*

The issue is not that of being narrow-minded or closed-minded, but of what is true. Nobody thinks it is narrow-minded to avoid poison. Eat poison and you die. That is the truth. The Bible presents Jesus as the only way—that is the truth.

A recent TV talk show had on a panel of leaders from various religions. Just before a commercial break, the confused host turned to the Christian minister who was on the panel and asked him, "Can't the Hindu go to heaven?" They broke to a commercial before he could give an answer.

The Hindu, just like anyone else, can go to heaven if he becomes a Christian by receiving Jesus as his Savior. However, there is one thing that the talk show host may not have realized when he asked his question. The Hindu does not want to go to heaven. There is no heaven in the Hindu religion. The talk show host had fallen into the error of *pluralism*. Pluralism is the belief that it is possible to blend all religions into one. Pluralism is the idea that we can cancel out certain beliefs that we do not agree with in order to form a more pleasing belief system.

If the essential elements were eliminated from the various religions, we would have a new religion of our own making. We would have committed a form of religious imperialism by robbing each of their vital teachings against the will of those who follow those teachings. For example, no Hindu would want to give up the belief in many gods or the belief in reincarnation. No Buddhist would be willing to give up the belief that there is no personal god. In the same way, it is not fair to try to eliminate the central core of what makes Christianity Christ-centered. Christianity plainly teaches that Jesus is the only way. The exclusivity of Christ is at the very center of Christianity. There can be no Christianity without the exclusive claims of Christ.

■ How can a God of love send anyone to hell?

Hell is *final* judgment. It is the final curtain call in God's plan for his creation. It is his last and final act of justice that brings human history to a close. This final judgment is called "the second death" (Revelation 20:14). Remember Adam and Eve? God said to them, *"When you eat of it you will surely die"* (Genesis 2:17). Every descendant from Adam, the whole human race, is born spiritually dead. This is followed by physical death. The second death is the final judgment of being sent to hell.

Love and justice cannot be separated. How could a loving God allow the multitude of horrendous acts that have occurred on this planet go unpunished? The universal cry of the human heart that has existed in every corner of this earth, and for all time, is the cry for justice. It is part of our very being. How then could we not expect God to be just?

Abraham cried out to God as God was about to bring judgment upon the city of Sodom, *"Will not the Judge of all the earth do right?"* (Genesis 18:25) If you will read the remainder of the account, you will find that an answer was given to Abraham that fully satisfied him. God is just, and his justice is absolutely perfect.

How would *we* choose to mete out justice? Perhaps we would start with the most wicked humans in history. There have been many world leaders such as emperors, kings, and dictators who have been responsible for the untold suffering and death of millions of people. Perhaps our justice should be focused on them.

Perhaps we should raise the bar of justice to included the multitude of mass murderers who have committed their unspeakable acts. Although they have not been involved in political intrigue, they have exacted their own brand of murderous intrigue on their helpless victims. Let them face our judgment.

Let's move the bar of justice a little higher to include people who have robbed and maimed, raped and pillaged innocent victims. Then we might want also to move the standard of justice to include ordinary criminals, abusers, neglectors and all the other social vandals of humanity. Soon, the question will have to arise, "Where will we draw the line?"

The answer is given in the Bible. *"All have sinned and fallen short of the glory of God"* (Romans 3:23). God's justice declares that all are under condemnation. Let's not forget that the very fact that we all die is due to God's judgment on sin. So, we actually live with God's judgment every day because all die. The fact that death exists in our world serves as a reminder that judgment on sin is a reality.

I know the answer to questions pertaining to love and justice can open the door to more questions, but let this answer begin to ease your mind that the "Judge of all the earth" will do right. To help you arrive at this place of trust, here's another question to ponder: "Why should God bother to save anyone at all?" If God saved just one person per century he could still be lauded as being loving and merciful.

However, the fact is, God takes no pleasure in the death of anyone and wants all people to come to salvation (Ezekiel 18:32; 2 Peter 3:9). He himself has paved the way by sending his Son to pay the *just* price for all people. Now the question becomes, who will bow to his will as it is revealed in the Bible?

Here are two quotes to ponder from two very highly esteemed Christian thinkers:

"The center of salvation is the cross of Jesus. And the reason it is so easy to obtain salvation is because it cost so much. The cross is the point where God and sinful man merge with a crash and the way of life is opened—but the crash is on the heart of God." [5]

---

5   Oswald Chambers, *My Utmost for His Highest* (Toronto: McClelland and Stewart Limited: 1935), 97.

"There will be only two kinds of people in the end: those who say to God, 'Thy will be done,' and those to whom God says, 'Thy will be done'" [6]

---

6   C.S. Lewis, *The Great Divorce* (New York: Collier Books: 1946), 72.

Chapter Five

THE CHURCH

KEY POINTS

- The church is not a building, but the people of God
- The people of God are representatives of Jesus Christ
- The role of the Holy Spirit in the church
- The mystery of the church's eternal covenant in its relationship to God

There are a lot of important organizations and institutions on earth. Some are civic, some are cultural, and some are political. There are entertainment entities like network television, cable, the motion picture industry, and symphony orchestras. There are sports conglomerates like the NFL, the NBA, and the PGA. There are huge financial and monetary organizations. Then the whole world is made up of nations. Some have been around for thousands of years. Now, consider the church. Out of all the organizations, institutions, and nations on the face of the earth, the church is the only one that will last forever.

We naturally put a lot of emphasis on the institutions of this world. It might be worth considering that many of our most stable and strong institutions have only been in existence for a short time. In fact, the United States is not yet 300 years old. What is it about the church that sets it apart? As you study this section you will gain some important insights that will forever change the way you view the church.

There are many ways to think about the church. We talk of going to church. We sit in church. There is the church on Third Avenue. What exactly is the church? In this chapter we will look at the biblical definition of the church. We will describe the church in four ways: (1) the people of God, (2) the body of Christ, (3) the temple of the Holy Spirit, and (4) the bride of Christ.

AFFILIATION ALERT

Some people want nothing to do with organized religion. They use this as an excuse to exempt themselves from the life of the local body of believers who meet regularly. Sadly, they lose the positive aspect of mutual accountability. A biblical orientation towards the church should lead to a deeper understanding and appreciation what mutual accountability means.

Everything else people are involved with requires organization. Imagine the insanity of going to an unorganized workplace or an unorganized hospital. Why select the church as having no need of organization? The church *is* organized. It is organized by God, led by the Holy Spirit with Jesus as the head. All people who belong to God should be concerned with their own involvement with God's church. This is an ALERT to prompt you to be willing to see the church in a whole new light—the light of God's Word.

Section One

THE PEOPLE OF GOD

Aren't all people God's people? Yes, everyone lives under the umbrella of God's creation. *"In him we live and move and have our being"* (Acts 17:28). Beyond this, however, not everyone lives under God's covenant. This covenant is both inclusive and exclusive. Those who are in a covenant relationship with God are, by the very definition of the covenant, God's people. All other people are categorically excluded. Let's begin by looking at examples from Israel's history.

Example from the Old Testament

God called out a people for himself from among all the people of the world. He began with Abraham and built a nation that would come to be known as Israel. This is why God could say to Pharaoh, "Let *my* people go." The concept that God would have a people he could call his own is repeated often in the Old Testament. *"I will walk among you and be your God and you will be my people"* (Leviticus 26:12). That God had a people he could call his own was a common refrain in the Old Testament:

For you are a people holy to the LORD your God. The LORD your God has chosen you out of all the peoples on the face of the earth to be his people, his treasured possession (Deuteronomy 7:6).

This sense of belonging was the driving force behind the covenant that God made with his people. It is what made the people who belonged to God the "people of God." It cannot be overemphasized that out of all the people on the face of the earth, these were God's people by his own declaration.

However, the people of God were unable to live up to the demands of the covenant. They were found to be unfaithful. Judgment fell on the people of God. The covenant was annulled because it was broken beyond repair. One example of the LORD's point of view can be found the book of Hosea:

When the LORD began to speak through Hosea, the LORD said to him, "Go, take to yourself an adulterous wife and children of unfaithfulness, because the land is guilty of the vilest adultery in departing from the LORD" (Hosea 1:2).

Hosea had children born to him and each of their names would carry prophetic implications for the people of God. One such child was named, "Lo-Ammi" (not mine). This prophet's child, along with the child's name, would serve as an object lesson for the people:

Then the LORD said, "Call him Lo-Ammi, for you are not my people, and I am not your God" (Hosea 1:9).

The marriage between God and his people was over. However, God's faithfulness would never die. He promised a future restoration that would come later with a New Covenant:

I will say to those called "Not my people," "You are my people"; and they will say, "You are my God" (Hosea 2:23).

This powerful prophecy was fulfilled through the work of Jesus Christ. Paul used this very passage from Hosea in Romans 9:25–26 to show that God keeps his promises.

Example from the New Testament

The promise of becoming "the people of God" would see its ultimate fulfillment in the New Covenant. The New Covenant would be put into effect through Jesus Christ. People who place their faith in Christ would now be the ones who belong to God through Jesus Christ.

"I will build my church and the gates of Hades will not overcome it" (Matthew 16:18).

We can learn a few things from this proclamation of Jesus. The first thing is that Jesus himself would build the church. It is important to realize that Jesus was not speaking of a physical building. He was speaking of people. *People* are the church. People are the ones called out of the world. The word for "church" in the Bible is the word *ekklessia—ek* (out)—*kaleō* (to call). It was a word that was used at the time for any group of people who were in assembly. It has been translated in our English Bibles from Old English as "church."

The people whom Jesus called out are his possession. "I will build *my* church" (called-out ones). Exactly how does he build his church? In the Old Testament a sign of the covenant was given to Abraham in Genesis 17. God was adamant that anyone, direct descendant or not, who did not receive the sign of the covenant would, therefore, not belong to him. They would be excluded. There were to be no exceptions:

"This is my covenant with you and your descendants after you, the covenant you are to keep: Every male among you shall be circumcised. You are to undergo circumcision, and it will be the sign of the covenant between me and you. From the generations to come every male among you who is eight days old must be circumcised, including those born in your household or bought with money from a foreigner—those who are not your offspring . . . My covenant in your flesh is to be an everlasting covenant. Any uncircumcised male, who has not been circumcised in the flesh, will be cut off from his people; he has broken the covenant" (Genesis 17:10–14).

Many of the laws and rituals in the Old Testament were to be fulfilled later through Christ. Circumcision was symbolic of the cutting away of the flesh, that is, the sinful nature of humanity. In the New Testament the outward symbol would become an inward reality. Paul spoke of what it meant to truly belong to God:

A man is not a Jew if he is only one outwardly, nor is circumcision merely outward and physical. No, a man is a Jew if he is one inwardly; and circumcision is circumcision of the heart, by the Spirit, not by the written code. Such a man's praise is not from men, but from God (Romans 2:28–29).

Paul related the outward ritual of circumcision by the hands of men to the inward reality of a different kind of circumcision *not* done by human hands. It was to be done by the Holy Spirit. This was a reference to the new birth that Jesus explained to Nicodemus in the third chapter of the Gospel of John.

Paul mentioned it again in Galatians. He wanted to move the emphasis away from some outward religious ritual. The new emphasis would be the reality of a new and living relationship to God:

Neither circumcision nor uncircumcision means anything; what counts is a new creation (Galatians 6:15).

Paul again referred to the sign of circumcision in his letter to the Colossian church:

In him you were also circumcised, in the putting off of the sinful nature, not with a circumcision done by the hands of men but with the circumcision done by Christ, having been buried with him in baptism and raised with him through your faith in the power of God, who raised him from the dead (Colossians 2:11–12).

There is a spiritual circumcision that must happen. It is the "cutting away" of our sinful flesh, which was symbolized in the Old Testament ritual of cutting away of the male foreskin. Under the New Covenant, a person is born again by the Holy Spirit. The old, sinful nature is "cut off," and a new nature is given. In his letter to the Colossians, Paul compared it to baptism. Baptism symbolizes our death and burial. Our old life is "cut off" (symbolized by being "buried" under the water). Then we are raised to new life by the power of the Holy Spirit (symbolized by being raised out of the water). This is all through the atoning work of Jesus Christ and his resurrection from the dead.

Once people have been born again, they are marked with a seal, not with an outward seal as represented in circumcision, but with the inward seal of the Holy Spirit:

And you also were included in Christ when you heard the word of truth, the gospel of your salvation. Having believed, you were marked in him with a seal, the promised Holy Spirit (Ephesians 1:13–14).

In order to be the "people of God" it is an absolute necessity that this blessed relationship be entered by means of the Holy Spirit. It must be in the way prescribed by God. It must be by placing our faith and trust in the One sent by God. This is the way we belong to God.

"You must be born again" (John 3:3). While this is inclusive: *"The Spirit himself testifies with our spirit that we are God's children,"* (Romans 8:16), it is also exclusive: *"If anyone does not have the Spirit of Christ he does not belong to Christ"* (Romans 8:9).

A Change in Our Thinking About the Church

The church belongs to Jesus and we (the church) belong to him. We must continuously recognize the fact that the true church is made up of people, not buildings or ecclesiastical organizations. Also, we must be aware of the fact that Jesus is Lord of the church. Jesus is *our* Lord.

TIME OUT

Believers have a calling. God has called us out of this world. We do not belong to this world anymore. We must learn to unlearn the world's ways. This is such a radical concept that it usually takes many years before believers ever realize this truth. In the meantime there may be conflicts between the way the world thinks and the way God would want us to think. This is a time out to have you read a passge of Scripture that may help build you up in the faith as you wrestle with your new calling.

Read John 15:18–27 slowly and carefully several times.

This passage is in the middle of Jesus' encouragement to his disciples in the book of John. It starts in chapter 14 and continues until the end of chapter 17. Read and meditate on what it means to be called out of the world and called into a different kingdom—the kingdom of God. We are promised the help of the Holy Spirit as we move forward in our relationship with the Lord in this world. We all must know the difference between the kingdom of this world and the kingdom of God. Conflict is guaranteed.

Section Two

THE BODY OF CHRIST

The church as the "body of Christ" speaks of three things: (1) our relationship to Christ, (2) our relationship to each other, and (3) our relationship to the world.

1. Our Relationship to Christ

Jesus is the head of the church. He has sovereignty over us. It was Jesus who had the authority to cleanse the temple in Jerusalem. This was something no one else could do. Jesus has the same authority today. In the first three chapters of Revelation Jesus demonstrated his authority as he walked through the lampstands of his church. He brought correction and exhortation. Jesus is sovereign over the church. Jesus is called "Lord" for that very reason:

And God placed all things under his feet and appointed him to be head over everything for the church, which is his body, the fullness of him who fills everything in every way (Ephesians 1:22–23).

2. Our Relationship to One Another

We are connected to each other in some amazing ways. We belong to Christ, and we belong to each other. We are united to one another by the Holy Spirit. We are all truly brothers and sisters in the Lord. This is not a man-made unity. It is a unity that cannot be forced or brought into being by a committee or mandated by decree. It can only come into existence by the power and work of the Holy Spirit:

The body is a unit, though it is made up of many parts; and though all its parts are many, they form one body. So it is with Christ. For we were all baptized by one Spirit into one body. . . .

Now the body is not made up of one part but of many. If the foot should say, "Because I am not a hand, I do not belong to the body," it would not for that reason cease to be part of the body. And if the ear should say, "Because I am not an eye, I do not belong to the body," it would not for that reason cease to be part of the body. If the whole body were an eye, where would the sense of hearing be? If the whole body were an ear, where would the sense of smell be? But in fact God has arranged the parts in the body, every one of them just as he wanted them to be. If they were all one part, where would the body be? As it is, there are many parts, but one body.

The eye cannot say to the hand, "I don't need you!" And the head cannot say to the feet, "I don't need you!" On the contrary, those parts of the body that seem to be weaker are indispensable, and the parts that we think are less honorable we treat with special honor. And the parts that are unpresentable parts are treated with special modesty, while our presentable parts need no special treatment. But God has combined the members of the body and has given greater honor to the parts that lacked it, so that there should be no division in the body, but that its parts should have equal concern for each other. If one part suffers, every part suffers with it; if one part is honored, every part rejoices with it. Now you are the body of Christ and each one of you is a part of it (1 Corinthians 12:12–27).

3. Our Relationship to the World

We, as the church, are made up of living human beings. We belong to each other. We need to begin to fit in to God's plan for the church as we relate to the world around us:

It was he who gave some to be apostles, some to be prophets, some to be evangelists, and some to be pastors and teachers, to prepare God's people for works of service, so that the body of Christ may be built up (Ephesians 4:11–12).

The emphasis is on being equipped for works of service. The idea is taken from the life of fishermen. They drag their nets on shore, and then they mend (prepare) them for service. Believers are, in a sense, pulled ashore—rescued from the world. Then it is the task of the church, with the help of God, to begin the mending (equipping) process so that we can be sent back out to impact the world for Christ.

We are not only the body of Christ in complete unity with each other, but we are the body of Christ as he makes his influence known in the world through us.

A Change in Our Thinking About the Church

An accurate view of the church will change our concept of what it is we are doing when we meet together on a typical Sunday or at any other time. We meet for a purpose. We are believers in the process of becoming equipped for works of service. A proper view of the church will cause us to jettison the spectator mentality that is so prevalent in our culture. We will *now* go to our meetings with an eye toward service. We are called to fulfill the will of the Lord for our lives. Worship and service will be united.

Section Three

THE TEMPLE OF THE HOLY SPIRIT

1. The Church Is Not a Natural Institution.

The church is a supernatural institution. It was instituted by God in Jesus Christ through the power of the Holy Spirit. We can read about the birth of the church as described in the second chapter of the book of Acts. It was born of the Holy Spirit at Pentecost. In a sense it can be said that *all* believers are "Pentecostals."

Don't you know that you yourselves are God's temple and that God's Spirit lives in you? (1 Corinthians 3:16)

Paul felt it necessary to remind the Corinthian church that they were no longer only under the influence of the natural world. There was a higher calling on their lives. He told them that believers were temples of the Holy Spirit. Paul wrote this to alert us that we have the power of the

Holy Spirit alive in us. It is the very power of the Holy Spirit working in and through the lives of those who belong to God through Jesus Christ:

And I will ask the Father, and he will give you another Counselor to be with you forever—the Spirit of truth. The world cannot accept him because it neither sees him nor knows him. But you know him, for he lives with you and will be in you (John 14:16–17).

Since the church is not a natural institution, we should use caution whenever we attempt to identify the church. The common way of identifying the church is to point to buildings and other man-made structures and organizations. We will be less prone to do this once we realize that the church is made up of *people* who are temples of the Holy Spirit.

We also might mistakenly think of the church as being some ecclesiastical institution endowed and sanctioned by human authority. Understanding that the church has supernatural foundations apart from the will of humanity will help to remove the usual human and political pitfalls that have occurred throughout history.

The church is an invisible entity and not subject to the usual sensual requirements normally associated with the word *church*. The church is not always going to be seen. There may be many surprises at the end of the age about the true identity of those who have been (or have not been) possessions of Christ. The church is not a natural, human organization.

2. <u>The Church Is Not the Church without the Holy Spirit</u>.

No one can belong to the true church of Jesus Christ without being born of the Holy Spirit. Jesus explained this to Nicodemus in John 3. Believers must be born of the Spirit into the church. Paul referred to believers as being new creations in Christ:

If anyone is in Christ, he is a new creation; the old has gone, the new has come! (2 Corinthians 5:17)

The true church, born of the Holy Spirit, exists without denomination. It exists without respect to geographical location, national, or ethnic boundaries. There is unity that can only come from being one in Christ through the sovereign power of the Holy Spirit. There may be differences in language and culture. There may be differences in how specific congregations or denominations choose to govern themselves, but *"...what counts is new creation"* (Galatians 6:15).

A Change In Our Thinking About the Church

The church is made up of born-again believers. It forms a living entity brought into being and sustained by the Holy Spirit regardless of outside appearances or national and political affiliation:

As you come to him, the living Stone—rejected by men but chosen by God and precious to him—you also, like living stones, are being built into a spiritual house (1 Peter 2:4–5).

But you are a chosen people, a royal priesthood, a holy nation, a people belonging to God . . . Once you were not a people, but now you are the people of God; once you had not received mercy, but now you have received mercy (1 Peter 2:9–10).

Section Four

THE BRIDE OF CHRIST

1. Intimacy In Relationship

There is an intimacy that speaks of the mysterious union between Christ and the church (believers). It is not a mystery in that it is unknowable, but it is a mystery in terms of complete human understanding. We remain tied to Christ in a most intimate way, yet we may at times feel quite far from him. We are related in the most intimate of terms, yet we may often feel that our lives do not reflect that intimacy. The fact that we may falter makes the fact of our relationship no less real. We may not fathom the depths of it all, but it is no less true. It remains a mystery.

There is no closer bond in human life than the bond of marriage. Paul spoke of this union and related it to union with Christ:

Husbands love your wives as Christ loved the church and gave himself up for her . . . For this reason a man shall leave his father and mother and be united with his wife and the two shall become one flesh. This is a profound mystery—but I am talking about Christ and the church (Ephesians 5:25; 32).

There is no other relationship that better portrays the intimacy between Christ and the church than that of the marriage of husband and wife. Let's remember that it was God himself who instituted and blessed the first marriage in the Garden of Eden. It was surely meant to reflect the image of God in his capacity for love and faithfulness.

The Old Covenant was often described in terms of the same fidelity that would be expected in marriage. God sent prophets again and again to correct his unfaithful people. There was a serious breach of fidelity that had occurred by their worship of other gods. In fact, it was spiritual adultery. The LORD used highly-charged emotional language in an effort to reach his people:

The word of the LORD came to me: "Go and proclaim in the hearing of Jerusalem: 'I remember the devotion of your youth, how as a bride you loved me and followed me through the desert.'" (Jeremiah 2:1–2).

"I gave faithless Israel her certificate of divorce and sent her away because of all her adulteries. Yet I saw that her unfaithful sister Judah had no fear; she also went out and committed adultery" (Jeremiah 3:8).

"Return, faithless people," declares the LORD, "for I am your husband" (Jeremiah 3:14).

God's covenant was one of faithfulness that demanded the same fidelity as that of a marriage. The people were unable to maintain right relationship, and the covenant was broken beyond repair. The lesson learned is that human beings are unable to be in right relationship with God because of the weaknesses inherent in fallen human nature. The New Covenant has a more secure ground because it is founded in the nature of another. Perfect faithfulness and fidelity can only be found in Christ. He will guarantee the ultimate fulfillment of the New Covenant.

2. Intimacy In the Future

The guarantee of intimacy in relationship with the Lord can often be overlooked, but it is one of the greatest blessings in the life of a believer. It is the constant, unbroken joy of fellowship with God—both in this life and in the next. Jesus gave gentle and tender words of encouragement for his disciples as he strengthened them for his departure:

Do not let your hearts be troubled. Trust in God; trust also in me. In my Father's house are many rooms; if it were not so, I would have told you. I am going there to prepare a place for you. And if I go and prepare a place for you, I will come back and take you to be with me that you also may be where I am (John 14:1–3).

The clear teaching of Scripture is that Jesus will return for his bride, the church. There is the promise of future fellowship that will result in the second coming of Christ. This will be the consummation of the age. The book of Revelation gives us the fulfillment of this promise:

Then I heard what sounded like a great multitude, like the roar of rushing waters and like loud peals of thunder, shouting: "Hallelujah! For our Lord God Almighty reigns. Let us rejoice and be glad and give him glory! For the wedding of the Lamb has come, and his bride has made herself ready. Fine linen, bright and clean was given her to wear." . . . Then the angel said to me, "Write: 'Blessed are those who are invited to the wedding supper of the Lamb!'" And he added, "These are the true words of God" (Revelation 19:6–9).

The future of the church is bright. It is beyond bright. There is nothing in this world to which it can be compared. Everything on earth will one day disappear, but the church—the people of God—will continue on forever in the presence of God:

The Spirit and the bride say, "Come!" And let him who hears say, "Come!" Whoever is thirsty, let him come; and whoever wishes, let him take the free gift of the water of life (Revelation 22:17).

The image of the church as the bride of Christ is the end goal of the great plan of salvation that God has for his creation. The bride of Christ has the privilege of being a part in the very invitation of God addressed to anyone willing to respond.

A Change In Our Thinking About the Church

The church is made up of organized pilgrims of incredible value. We are organized by God and called to be pilgrims while on an earthly journey toward heaven. We are of incredible value to God, proven by the fact that he would send his own Son to buy our pardon. We will be with him forever. Such is the destiny of the church, the bride of Christ.

TIME OUT

Go over all four perspectives: (1) the people of God, (2) the body of Christ, (3) the temple of the Holy Spirit, and (4) the bride of Christ. Think deeply and meditate on these four biblical portraits of the church.

Try to give examples (using Scripture references) from each biblical description of the church. Make a chart showing what Scriptures point to the church as being the people of God, the body of Christ, the temple of the Holy Spirit, and the bride of Christ. As you take the time to chart these four characteristics of the church, you will be blessed. The church will never again be seen as merely some sort of building or some earthly social institution.

CONCLUSION

The church is part of God's divine plan of redemption. We need to be extra cautious and not allow ourselves to slip into the world's way of thinking. The church is God's redeemed community living between the time of the resurrection of Jesus and his second coming. The true believer is to be involved in those things in which God is involved. God is highly involved in his church. The true believer is to be invested in those things in which God is invested. He has invested his best in the church, Jesus Christ.

STUDY QUESTIONS

1.   Can you give an Old Testament example of the concept, "The people of God?"

2.   Can you give a New Testament example of the ultimate fulfillment of the concept, "The people of God?"

3.   How would you describe the relationship of the church to Jesus Christ based on the church being called the body of Christ?

4.   How are the individual members of the church affected by being called the body of Christ?

5.   How would you describe what is meant by the two terms, "visible" church and the "invisible" church?

6.   How does one become a member of the church?

7.   Can you cite three or four New Testament references to the church being joined with Christ at his second coming?

QUESTIONS PEOPLE ASK

■ *Do I have to go to church to be a Christian?*

No. Remember, if you are a believer, *you* are the church. You may never set foot in a church building. However, meeting together regularly with other believers is God's plan. A believer should want to be a part of God's plan. We are admonished in the Bible to meet together as a means of carrying out God's will for his church:

Let us consider how we may spur one another on toward love and good deeds. Let us not give up meeting together, as some are in the habit of doing, but let us encourage one another—and all the more as you see the Day approaching (Hebrews 10:24–25).

So much more can happen as we meet together than if we stay separated and alone. The potential is endless. However, those who stay away restrict what God wants to do in us and through us.

Meeting with other believers is not merely "going to church." Remember, the purpose for being involved in a church is to be in the process of becoming equipped for works of service. Sometimes people may struggle staying involved and active in a church. It is God's will us that we do the best we can to yield to his will. God's will is stated in the following verse:

"And he died for all, that those who live should no longer live for themselves but for him who died for them and was raised again" (2 Corinthians 5:15).

Chapter Six

THE TRINITY

- The Bible reveals the nature of God.
- The Bible reveals the doctrine of the Trinity.
- It is helpful to understand the history of the arguments regarding the Trinity.

We serve a God that can be known

God is absolutely transcendent. He is infinitely beyond our comprehension. However, the fact of his transcendence does not mean that we can know nothing about him. We will never know *all* that there is to know about God, but we can know some things about him. First of all, the Bible clearly states that we can know about God by looking at his creation:

For since the creation of the world God's invisible qualities—his eternal power and divine nature—have been clearly seen, being understood from what has been made, so that men are without excuse (Romans 1:20).

Besides creation, we can also know God through our conscience:

Indeed, when Gentiles, who do not have the law, do by nature things required by the law, they are a law for themselves, even though they do not have the law, since they show that the requirements of the law are written on their hearts, their consciences also bearing witness, and their thoughts now accusing, now even defending them (Romans 2:14–15).

The two ways of knowing God in Romans 1 and 2 have often been termed *general revelation*. General revelation is open to all and is described as the revelation of nature and the revelation of conscience. Everyone is able to know something about God in these two ways. However, the revelation in nature and our conscience leaves many questions about the nature of God unanswered. God has helped in this difficulty by giving us his own revelation of himself. This is called *special revelation*. This special revelation is Scripture—the Bible. Without the special revelation of Scripture, there can be much confusion about the nature of God. God has graciously made himself known through his Word.

The biblical revelation of God is that he is *triune*. God is three in unity. The term triune means that God is one being, existing in three distinct co-equal, co-eternal persons: Father, Son, and Holy Spirit. We are not saying that God is three beings *and* one being. To say this would be a contradiction. God is one being and three persons. We are not saying that God is three persons *and* one person. Again, that would be a contradiction. God is three persons and one being. Another way to state this is to say that God is one "what" (nature and essence) and three "whos" (persons).

There is absolute distinction between persons (who) and absolute unity in the one being (what). Each person in the Godhead is not one-third God; each is one hundred percent God—unity in nature, plurality in person: triune (the Trinity).

God may be a mystery to our minds but knowledge of him is not irrational. God may be completely beyond us but not completely unknowable. God is transcendent but has made himself known. This chapter will make clear the important biblical revelation of the nature of the triune God.

ABSTRACT ALERT

A careful study of the nature of God is of utmost importance to all believers. We grow when we attend to the importance of this topic even though it may be a difficult one. While it may seem abstract and theoretical, it is bedrock, biblical truth. The more we wrestle with the biblical revelation of the essence and nature of God, the deeper our relationship with God will grow.

We will also find that most of the dangerous religious cults have embraced a wrong view of the nature of God. This supports that understanding the nature of God is not merely the study of some abstract theory, but deals with knowing a concrete reality that has the potential to affect the lives of everyone. This is an ALERT to encourage everyone to take the time and effort to understand the correct biblical revelation of the nature of God.

Section One

THREE PLATFORMS

The doctrine of the Trinity belongs to all of Christianity for the simple and basic reason that it is revealed in Scripture. It is part of the special revelation of God through his Word. We would not know the nature of God as triune without the revelation contained in the Bible. There are three platforms that form the foundation for the revelation of the Trinity: monotheism, three persons, and equality.

<u>Monotheism</u>

The Bible clearly makes the declaration that there is only one God:

Hear, O Israel: The LORD our God, the LORD is one (Deuteronomy 6:4).

This is the famous Hebrew *Shema*, which means, "Listen!" or "Hear!" It forms the most basic instructional unit pertaining to the knowledge of the nature of God. Jesus affirmed this fact when he was asked about the most important commandment of all:

"The most important one" answered Jesus, *"is this: 'Hear, O Israel, the Lord our God, the Lord is one'"* (Mark 12:29).

This is the most important commandment because it serves as the basis for true worship. The Ten Commandments begin with this same emphasis:

"You shall have no other gods before me" (Exodus 20:3).

Mono (one) theism (God) is the foundational doctrine of the Trinity, and it forms the first platform in the biblical revelation of the Trinity. Monotheism is unmistakably affirmed in both the Old and New Testaments.

Three Persons

There are, within the one being (God), three distinct persons. In the Old Testament, the holy nature that belongs to God alone was also indirectly ascribed to the Spirit of God. In creation we read that *"the Spirit of God was hovering over the waters"* (Genesis 1:2). We find in Scripture that God repeatedly sent the Holy Spirit to empower and enable his servants. We know that the Spirit of the LORD came upon King David in power, but the Spirit of the LORD had departed from Saul (1 Samuel 16:13–14). David would later pray, *"Do not cast me from your presence or take your Holy Spirit from me"* (Psalm 51:11). The prophet Isaiah recounted the instances of God's love toward Israel: *"Yet they rebelled and grieved his Holy Spirit"* (Isaiah 63:10). In the last days God has promised to *"pour out my Spirit on all people"* (Joel 2:28).

Besides the evidence of the Spirit of God, there are also indications that there was a specially anointed servant (Messiah) who was to come. He has been given divine names and attributes, yet he seemed to be distinct in identity from God himself. There are many references that can be cited:

For to us a child is born, to us a son is given, and the government will be on his shoulders. And he will be called Wonderful Counselor, Mighty God, Everlasting Father, Prince of Peace. Of the increase of his government and peace there will be no end. He will reign on David's throne and over his kingdom, establishing and upholding it with justice and righteousness from that time on and forever. The zeal of the Almighty God will accomplish this (Isaiah 9:6–7).

[The LORD] says, "It is too small a thing for you to be my servant to restore the tribes of Jacob and bring back those of Israel I have kept. I will also make you a light for the Gentiles, that you may bring my salvation to the ends of the earth (Isaiah 49:6).

"In my vision at night I looked, and there before me was one like a son of man, coming with the clouds of heaven. He approached the Ancient of Days and was led into his presence. He was given authority, glory and sovereign power; all people, nations and men of every language worshiped him. His dominion is an everlasting dominion that will not pass away, and his kingdom is one that will never be destroyed (Daniel 7:13–14).

"But you, Bethlehem Ephrathah, though you are small among the clans of Judah, out of you will come for me one who will be ruler over Israel, whose origins are from old, from ancient times" (Micah 5:2).

It is clear from the Old Testament that the Spirit of God and the ruler to come (the Messiah) were given the prerogatives and names of God. While this may not be all too explicit in the Old Testament, it set the stage for a fuller revelation in the New Testament.

In the New Testament we have a very clear revelation that uncovers what was alluded to in the Old Testament. The New Testament confirms that there are three distinct persons (yet one being) with all the features that would allow for personhood.

There are three instances recorded in the New Testament where one or more of the persons of the Trinity can be seen as active at the same time and in the same location.

At the baptism of Jesus, all *three* persons of the Godhead were represented:

As soon as Jesus was baptized, he went up out of the water. At that moment heaven was opened, and he saw the Spirit of God descending like a dove and lighting on him. And a voice from heaven said, "This is my Son, whom I love; with him I am well pleased" (Matthew 3:16–17).

There were two other times where the Father could be heard audibly speaking from heaven in the presence of Jesus and other witnesses. Once was at the transfiguration of Jesus: *"While [Peter] was still speaking, a bright cloud enveloped them, and a voice from the cloud said, 'This is my Son, whom I love; with him I am well pleased. Listen to him'"* (Matthew 17:5). The other time was when Jesus entered Jerusalem. Jesus prayed: *"Father, glorify your name!" Then a voice came from heaven, "I have glorified it, and I will glorify it again"* (John 12:28). We can also read of Jesus praying to the Father. Jesus spoke of returning to his Father and of sitting at his Father's right hand in heaven.

It is interesting that Jesus used the Old Testament law (Deuteronomy 17:6), which declared that two separate witnesses were needed to validate a claim. This could only be possible if God the Son and God the Father were two separate persons:

In your own law it is written that the testimony of two men is valid. I am one who testifies for myself; my other witness is the Father, who sent me" (John 8:17–18).

A great unifying declaration can also be seen as Jesus gave the Great Commission: *"Therefore go and make disciples of all nations, baptizing them in the name of the Father and of the Son and of the Holy Spirit"* (Matthew 28:19). Notice that all three persons of the Godhead are under the one name (authority) that makes up the fullness of the Godhead.

These examples make it clear that the true biblical revelation of the nature of God is that he exists in three distinct persons (whos), yet in one unified being (what).

Equality

The equality of the three persons within the one Godhead means that each member has full deity. The deity of the Father should be self-explanatory. The deity of the Son was covered in the chapter on Jesus Christ. The Bible clearly teaches the full deity of Christ. Let's take a look at the Holy Spirit.

The Holy Spirit is not an "it." The Holy Spirit is a person. It may be difficult to think of a being without a body as being a person. God is spirit, but he has personhood. Angels are spirits, but they have personhood. When our loved ones die, they no longer have a body, but they still have personhood. The Holy Spirit exhibits all the characteristics of personhood. He has intelligence: he knows the mind of God (1 Corinthians 2:11). He has emotion: he can be grieved (Ephesians 4:30). He has a will: he directed the activities of the church (Acts 8:29; 10:19; 16:6). The Holy Spirit prays for us, directs us, and still teaches us today (Romans 8:26; 1 John 2:27).

The Holy Spirit is not a blind force that can be manipulated by someone claiming to have some great spiritual power. This is because the Holy Spirit is a person, not a mindless force to be manipulated. Those who make the error of referring to the Holy Spirit as some kind of mindless spiritual force are not conveying the truth about the nature and character of the third person of the Trinity.

We can learn two important lessons from understanding the true nature of the Holy Spirit. First, we should not allow ourselves to be misled by people who treat the Holy Spirit of God as a force that they have somehow tamed. Who tames God? God the Father is sovereign, and so is God the Holy Spirit. The second lesson is that God's will and the will of the Holy Spirit are inseparable. Nothing is going to occur by the power of the Holy Spirit that is not in line with God's will. We can trust in the power of the Holy Spirit to bring God's will into our lives without thinking that we have been given over to some ethereal, non-personal force.

Besides having personhood, the Holy Spirit has full deity with all the attributes of God as well. He is eternal (Hebrews 9:14), omniscient (1 Corinthians 2:10–11), omnipresent (Psalm 139:7) and HOLY. The Holy Spirit was involved in creation itself (Genesis 1:2). When Peter was berating Ananias for lying to the Holy Spirit he said, *"You have not lied to men, but to God"* (Acts 5:4). Things are said about the Holy Spirit that can only be said of God.

The fact that the Holy Spirit plays a role that seems to be quietly behind the scenes by no means indicates that he is in any way less than God. Jesus took on an additional nature at his incarnation that allowed him to be vastly different than either the Father or the Spirit, yet Jesus remained fully God. The Holy Spirit will forever share the name of God as Jesus revealed to us in the giving of the Great Commission: *"baptizing in the name of the Father and of the Son and of the Holy Spirit"* (Matthew 28:19).

TIME OUT

Take time out to review the three platforms upon which the biblical teaching of the Trinity rests. These three platforms are contrasted with three common misunderstandings of the nature of God as revealed in the Bible.

1. MONOTHEISM: There is only one God

   ■ Monotheism is counter to polytheism–that there are many gods

2. EQUALITY: The Father, the Son and the Holy Spirit are equal in nature and essence

   ■ Equality is counter to subordinationism–that the Son and/or the Holy Spirit are less than God the Father

3. THREE PERSONS: The Father, the Son and the Holy Spirit are three distinct persons

   ■ Three Persons is counter to modalism–that God has, at certain times in history, taken on different modes of existence–one time he was the Father, and at another time he was the Son and at another time he was the Holy Spirit.

Section Two

THREE PROBLEMS IN COMMUNICATION

It seems whenever the discussion turns toward the Trinity, communication becomes difficult. Many times it is hard to get beyond the misconceptions that people have regarding the Trinity. The conversation often ends up going in circles rather than zeroing in on the truth. Three common problems are (1) misunderstanding, (2) analogy breakdown, and (3) the fact people might be uncomfortable with mystery.

1. Misunderstanding

Many people think that those who believe in the Trinity believe in three gods. We need to make sure they understand that this is *not* what we mean by the Trinity. The Bible explicitly teaches that there is only one God. Remember that the first platform in presenting the Trinity is monotheism. Monotheism is the most basic concept of the nature of God. The Bible clearly teaches that there is a Trinity, but that God is one.

Another problem often encountered is that the word "Trinity" is not found in the Bible. This fact is often used to negate the teaching regarding the Trinity. We must subject ourselves to the revelation of the Bible. It would be an error to reject the plain teaching of Scripture for the lack of one word. The concept of the Trinity is clearly revealed in the Bible. We use the word *Trinity* to represent the concept. If we do away with the word, it would not do away with the biblical truth surrounding the use of that word. The word *Trinity* is not found in the Bible, yet we do indeed have the concept.

There is also the misunderstanding that since the Holy Spirit seems to have a less prominent role, that it must follow somehow that he is not worthy of equal status with God. This would be an error. Because one or the other members of the Godhead happen to assume different roles does not constitute inferiority. The Father planned our salvation: he sent his Son. The Son accomplished our salvation: he died on the cross. The Holy Spirit then applies our salvation: he works in us so we can be born again. The different roles taken by the Father, Son, and Holy Spirit do not cause any one of them to lose full divine status. A deeper look into Scripture will show that their roles often overlap and that they also share the divine titles.

	FATHER	**SON**	**HOLY SPIRIT**
God	1 Peter 1:2	Romans 9:5	Acts 5:3–4
Omnipresent	1 Kings 8:27	Matthew 28:20	Psalm 139:7
Omniscient	Psalm 147:5	John 16:30	1 Corinthians 2:10
Omnipotent	Psalm 135:6	Matthew 28:18	Romans 15:19
Holy	Revelation 15:4	Acts 3:14	Romans 1:4
Eternal	Psalm 90:2	Micah 5:2	Hebrews 9:14
Truth	John 7:28	Revelation 3:7	1 John 5:6
Lord	Luke 2:11	Romans 10:12	2 Corinthians 3:17
Creator	Acts 14:15	Colossians 1:16	Job 33:4

This chart demonstrates that the Bible gives divine attributes to each of the three persons. The doctrine of the Trinity fits perfectly with the biblical revelation. It is easy to get lost in misleading arguments and faulty reasoning. The best way of coming to an understanding of the Trinity is to let Scripture speak for itself.

2. Analogy Breakdown

There have been many efforts to communicate the reality of the triune God by making him analogous to something. Perhaps you've heard the analogy of water, water vapor, and ice. Maybe you've heard the analogy of the eggshell, the yolk, and the egg-white. Some have tried to show the triune nature of God by using the analogy of time: past, present, and future. These analogies do show some form of a three-in-one relationship, but they fail to show the absolute complete unity and equality that is true for the biblical revelation of the triune nature of God.

Mathematical analogies have been tried. $1 + 1 + 1 = 3$ is a little weak. $1 \times 1 \times 1 = 1$ is a little better. Augustine tried the analogy of love. He said the Father is the lover, the Son is the beloved and the Holy Spirit is love. We should be careful with analogies because they do not give a completely accurate description of God. God is altogether unique. There is no adequate analogy for the nature of God. The best way to come to an understanding is to let the Bible speak for itself. Anything we may yet desire to know will have to remain a mystery. This leads us to the third problem to consider.

3. Mystery

There is no analogy that can adequately describe God in all his fullness. There is no other being like him. If we could completely understand God, then we would be his equal. We cannot completely understand the concept of infinity and yet we don't reject the concept. We shouldn't reject the biblical revelation of God because we cannot completely understand it. There is a mysterious element that exists when it comes to the full extent that we can know God.

There is mystery involved in our knowledge of God, yet we can still know him. God has made himself known to us specifically through his Word. We can also know God through our relationship of being born of the Spirit. We must be careful not to engage in undue speculation that goes beyond what has been revealed in Scripture concerning the nature of God. All teaching about God must have a solid biblical foundation.

God is greater than we are, so much greater that it defies description except to say that he is infinitely greater than us in every way. Therefore, there will always be an element of mystery. This is cause for rejoicing because we serve a God who is holy and transcendent, yet has graciously chosen to reveal himself to us. We are promised a closer view and more understanding after the return of Christ:

"Now we see but a poor reflection as in a mirror; then we shall see face to face. Now I know in part; then I shall know fully, even as I am known" (1 Corinthians 13:12).

Section Three

THREE PERSONS IN CHURCH HISTORY

The teaching in the Scriptures about one God in three Persons existed before formal creeds were written by ecclesiastical institutions. Even so, some people attempt to teach that the Trinity was a doctrine that was forced on the church some 400 years or so after the time of Christ. The doctrine of the Trinity was already a clear biblical revelation before the formal creeds came into existence.

From the very beginning, the collected believers had many difficulties just surviving in the culture. There was overt hostility, and it seemed that the church was often running for its life. There was no time to formalize teaching or to set the basic tenets of the faith in a convenient creedal form. Three characters in church history had a major influence in this very important time. They were Emperor Constantine, Arius, and Athanasius.

Constantine was the emperor of the Roman Empire around A.D. 300. He had a very strong desire to bring unity to the empire. The events surrounding the persecution of Christians were a hindrance to the unity he sought. He issued an edict in the year 313 that brought the blatant persecution of Christians to a stop. Some say he issued the edict because he himself had become a Christian. Others say that we cannot be too sure, but what was true was that he wanted a unified Roman Empire. Furthermore, he had discovered that within the Christian church itself there was discord.

There was a certain pastor in the city of Alexandria, Egypt, who taught that Jesus Christ was not equal with God and that Jesus was a creation of God. His name was Arius. Arius was a clever man and had a way with words (and public opinion). He utilized slogans that gave his idea favor with the people. One such slogan was, "There was a time when the Son was not." Arius persuaded a vast number of believers to his position. We already know how difficult the doctrine of the Trinity is to understand, much less to explain. Imagine how hard it must have been for the average believer in that day who did not have access to a Bible. Furthermore, the doctrine of the Trinity sounded too much like the pagan polytheistic religions out of which they had just come. They couldn't figure the deity of Christ into the scheme of things. To think of Jesus as a created being made more sense to them from a natural point of view. The battle for the biblical revelation was about to begin.

Emperor Constantine wanted to put an end to the controversy. He called a council of the church leaders. He convened the meeting himself in the city of Nicea in A.D. 325 and then left it up to the theologians to come to an understanding on of the deity of Christ. The issue of the deity of Christ is central to the doctrine of the Trinity. At the council of Nicea there was much heated discussion, and ultimately the Arian position was defeated, but Arius was not defeated. He continued to pursue his view of Christ wherever he went.

There was a young deacon from Alexandria present at the council by the name of Athanasius. He was an assistant to the bishop of Alexandria at that time, but he would very soon become bishop of Alexandria himself. Athanasius fought boldly for the acceptance of the full deity of Christ at the council of Nicea and continued to do so when he became bishop of Alexandria. However, the politics of the time would not allow Athanasius peace. He had to flee for his life because those in power were still persuaded that the Arian view regarding Christ was the correct one. The decision at the council of Nicea had failed to ease the situation entirely. Athanasius was banished from one city after another.

Athanasius fought for truth without giving up for more than fifty years until his death in 373. It wasn't until the council in Constantinople, in 381, where the doctrine of the full deity of Christ, as well as the doctrine of the deity of the Holy Spirit, were finally accepted as being taught in the Bible. We owe much to the tenacity and faithfulness of Athanasius who stood for biblical truth despite a whole world that seemed to be against him.

Church history makes for very interesting study. We have had creeds over the course of church history that have helped to clarify biblical doctrines, but the fight for biblical truth will never end. There are still groups today, even organizations that call themselves Christian, that believe neither in the deity of Christ, nor in the Trinity.

We don't believe in the doctrine of the Trinity because it happens to be a creedal statement. We believe in the doctrine of the Trinity because it is revealed in the Bible. The creeds are merely formalized statements about truths that already exist in Scripture. The history of the early church shows us that this battle for Scriptural truth is nothing new and will always be with us. Just as false worship is a reality going all the way back to Genesis, unbiblical teachings will be with us all the way to the end of the age. Our duty is to be able to use the Scriptures to discern truth from error.

Creeds must be used with caution. Creeds can become formal, complex, and abstract. They can be superimposed on Scripture. Properly handled, however, creeds facilitate public confession, form a succinct basis for teaching, safeguard pure doctrine, and constitute an appropriate focus for the believers' fellowship in the faith. Take a look at the creed of Nicea.

THE NICENE CREED: COUNCIL OF NICEA — A.D. 325

I believe in one God the Father Almighty; Maker of heaven and earth, and of all things visible and invisible.

And in one Lord Jesus Christ, the only-begotten Son of God, begotten of the Father before all worlds [God of God] light of light, very God of very God, begotten, not made, being of one substance [essence] with the Father; by whom all things were made; who, for us men and for our salvation, came down from heaven, and was incarnate by the Holy Ghost of the Virgin Mary, and was made man; and was crucified also for us under Pontius Pilate; He suffered and was buried; and the third day He rose again, according to the Scriptures; and ascended into heaven, and sitteth on the right hand of the Father;

and He shall come again, with glory, to judge both the quick and the dead; whose kingdom shall have no end.

And [I believe] in the Holy Ghost, the Lord and Giver of life; who proceedeth from the Father [and the Son]; who with the Father and the Son together is worshipped and glorified; who spake by the Prophets. And [I believe] in the Holy Catholic and Apostolic church. I acknowledge one Baptism for the remission of sins; and I look for the resurrection of the dead, and the life of the world to come. Amen.

Note: The last paragraph was added at Constantinople in A.D. 381.

Section Four

THREE REASONS WHY TRUTH IS IMPORTANT

There can be an attitude of laxity, or even apathy, when it comes to truth. Sometimes the tendency of human nature is to take the least painful route. It might seem to be less painful just to let things be and allow truth to find its own way. However, once we become believers, our spiritual eyes are opened. We may often find ourselves in a fight for the truth. Truth becomes important because we serve the God of truth.

The following three reasons demonstrate why truth about the nature of God is important. Obviously, it was important to the early church and to men like Athanasius. It should be important to us as well.

1. Truth Honors God

Jesus said, *"God is spirit, and his worshipers must worship in spirit and in truth"* (John 4:24). God must be worshiped for who he has revealed himself to be. There are many misconceptions about the nature of God because there are many people who have not received their knowledge of God from the Bible. Failure to accept the Bible as our only source of truth about the nature of God only opens the door for other sources of questionable authority.

Any idea about the nature of God that falls short of God's own revelation falls short of reality. It is not the truth. If it is not the truth, then it dishonors God. People may be very sincere, but it still doesn't make them immune from error. The truth about God is honoring to him, and he himself has put a tremendous amount of emphasis on this fact.

2. Errors Lead to More Errors.

Many non-Christian religions and cults commenced by having false ideas about the true nature of God. They hold to views of God completely foreign to the Bible. Some of them have embraced the idea that there are many gods. Some have even taught that we ourselves are gods. Others have taught that God is too transcendent to be known or that he is a mere impersonal force.

Some have false ideas about the nature and character of Jesus Christ. To many people Jesus was some kind of highly evolved spirit-man. To others Jesus was just one of many prophets who have come. As a result, many people have relegated Jesus to the level of a mere created being.

There are people who have the false idea about the Holy Spirit. To them he is just some kind of force. They have the mistaken idea that, with a little of the right kind of spiritual hocus-pocus, a highly skilled person can learn to manipulate the Holy Spirit.

Once an error of any kind is introduced, it isn't long before more errors will appear. Inevitably there will be attitudes, actions, and behaviors that might lead to sin or to dangerous practices. But the gravest danger of all is that it will also confound the salvation message of the Bible.

3. Truth Intensifies Worship and Strengthens Faith.

Full and accurate knowledge of the nature of God will strengthen our faith. Our confidence will increase, and we will be better versed at communicating the truth about God to others. Our faith in God will expand when we have a clearer understanding of who God is and what he has done.

We will be able to appreciate the Bible to an even greater degree when we realize that the Holy Spirit was behind its inspiration (2 Peter 1:21). The fact that our body is the temple of the Holy Spirit will take on much more importance (1 Corinthians 6:19). We will marvel at the fact that Jesus said he would send another comforter to be with us forever (John 14:16). When we read the book of Acts and learn how much the Holy Spirit directed the church, our appreciation for the third person of the Trinity will increase. This same Holy Spirit is at work in our lives today.

As we become more aware of the true identity of Jesus, think how much more we will be able to value his work of atonement on the cross. Think of the power and majesty of his person and work, his teaching, his holy example, and his love. To know that Jesus is our high priest, our shepherd, our redeemer, our Savior, and Lord will cause us to lift our voices in praise and adoration. Our adoration will increase all the more as we learn of his true divine status.

CONCLUSION

The Bible tells us that the full nature of God was involved in creation. God in all his glory is also involved in new creation:

Therefore, if anyone is in Christ, he is a new creation; the old has gone, the new has come! (2 Corinthians 5:17).

The world is full of people dedicated to the study of God's creation. We have astronomers, physicists, biologists, botanists, and zoologists, and the list goes on. We have barely begun to understand the grandeur that is God's handiwork. With this in mind, is it any wonder that we struggle to understand the God behind it all? We should not presume that we might corner him by some mathematical formula or some other clever means not found in the Bible. We can know and understand him as he has revealed himself to us. In response to this revelation, we bow and commit ourselves. We study him with reverence and awe as people who worship the One who is infinitely greater than all of creation itself. Blessed Trinity indeed.

STUDY QUESTIONS

1. The revelation of nature and the revelation of conscience tell us something about the nature of God. What is *special revelation* and why is special revelation important in informing us about the nature of God?

2. What is the first platform in discussing the nature of the Trinity?

3. What are the second and third platforms?

4. Can you cite some Old Testament passages that tell of the deity of the Holy Spirit and the deity of the Messiah?

5. Can you cite some New Testament passages that do the same?

6. What are the three categories discussed that might hinder communication about the Trinity?

7. What were the differences between Arius and Athanasius in how they each viewed the Trinity?

8. What are the three reasons why the truth about the nature of God is important?

Chapter Seven

DISCIPLESHIP

KEY POINTS

- We are called to God's mission of training and nurturing so we may be useful in his kingdom.

     We are called to be disciples.
- We who get involved in God's mission will not be left to ourselves.

     Jesus has promised to be with us — even to the end of the age.
- We will be on a life-long learning curve and will even sometimes fail.

     God has given us glorious freedom due to our relationship with him through Christ.

What is discipleship? It is an old word used to describe a very vital relationship. It doesn't mean we must all wear robes and say "thee" and "thou." It comes from the word *discipline*, which is a description of a student in a training relationship. Think for a moment what it means for someone in the medical profession to study the *discipline* of medicine. They have voluntarily placed themselves under the rigorous training necessary to carry out their duties in the best possible manner. A credible medical career would be impossible (and unthinkable) without this disciplined approach.

The same can be said of the various trades that have apprenticeship programs to train people in the knowledge and skills necessary to successfully ply a trade. A disciple can be thought of as a type of apprentice. A disciple is apprenticed to God.

God's desire is that the people who are in relationship with him be subject to his discipline and training. This is called discipleship.

Believers are invited into the most exciting and exhilarating part of their relationship to God. A healthy life in discipleship/training with the Lord will lead to the most blessed of lives. Discipleship is part of God's mission.

Section One

GOD'S MISSION

We may find it easy to think of people as being on a mission, but do we ever think of the fact that God is on a mission? His mission can be seen as the connecting thread that runs from Genesis through Revelation. His mission is to redeem what was lost to sin and to restore all things.

A Continuous Mission

God has been on this mission of redemption ever since the fall in the Garden of Eden. It is a mission of redemption that can be seen everywhere in Scripture. God called Abraham at the very beginning and said, *"all the peoples on earth will be blessed through you"* (Genesis 12:3). As God's redemptive history proceeded we can see his plan interwoven throughout the Scriptures.

His mission continued through Abraham, Isaac, and Jacob. Yet, it seemed time and time again that his plan would self-destruct. God's people were far from perfect. It was as if sabotage was the rule and disobedience the way. However, the secret to God's mission was that its success did not rest in human hands. Just as one of God's chosen human instruments came close to having everything dissolve into failure, God worked his gracious power. His plan would not fail. Why? It was *his* plan and *his* mission.

Even foreign nations couldn't stand in the way of God's plan of redemption. When the Egyptian Pharaoh tried to stop God's plan, the Pharaoh was defeated. The Pharaoh held a whole nation in brutal slavery for 400 years. As far as the people knew, their situation would last forever. It was an impossible situation, but with God nothing is impossible. This point has been proven over and over again. All we have to do is read God's history in dealing with his people as recorded in the Bible. God's mission was unrelenting even in the face of the most outrageous human failure and never-ending foreign interference.

God's mission would continue through David. King David was enjoying unsurpassed success. While he had spent much time and energy building a palace for himself, he realized that God needed a house. However, what would God do with a house when all of heaven and earth belonged to him? God had to remind David that it was *he* who gave him his success and that no one was more zealous for the mission of God than God himself:

The LORD declares to you that the LORD himself will establish a house for you; when your days are over and you rest with your fathers, I will raise up your offspring to succeed you, who will come from your own body, and I will establish his kingdom. He is the one who will build a house for my name, and I will establish the throne of his kingdom forever. I will be his father, and he will be my son (2 Samuel 7:11–14).

This episode in the life of David reminds us that God has a plan and a mission beyond what most people realize. David was thinking too small. He had to be instructed that God had eternal plans that went well beyond David's simple, temporal, and earthbound concerns. God had his mind on an eternal dynasty (house) headed up by the Son of David—the promised Messiah.

Many more accounts could be cited from Old Testament history where it was shown that God had an eternal plan that would supersede all other plans. God's ceaseless mission was pointing to its ultimate fulfillment in Jesus Christ.

A Costly Mission

While God's mission was (and still is) continuous, it was also very costly. Who can calculate the cost of God's own Son? We don't have any way of coming close to really understanding what it cost God or what it cost Jesus Christ. How do you measure infinite value?

God so loved the world that he GAVE his one and only Son... (John 3:16).

Make no mistake that this was *God's* mission. It cost him everything. He held nothing back. Even though we cannot fathom the cost, we must consider it. The more we think and meditate on what it cost God, the more we will come to understand the value that he places on his mission. This will also help us to more fully realize the priority God places on his mission as it affects our lives.

His mission is never ending, and it cost him a price that cannot be measured by any human standard. This mission is important to God. It should be of equal importance to those who are called by his name. God's mission will lead us into God's commission.

Section Two

GOD'S COMMISSION

Matthew 28 records the last words of Jesus. This has been called "The Great Commission."

All authority in heaven and on earth has been given to me. Therefore go and make disciples of all nations, baptizing them in the name of the Father and of the Son and of the Holy Spirit, and teaching them to obey everything I have commanded you. And surely I am with you always, to the very end of the age (Matthew 28:18–20).

TIME OUT

There have been great moments in history—so momentous that the slightest reference can lead people into a treasure trove of memories and associations: Pearl Harbor, D-Day, JFK, the lunar landing, 9/11. The memories and the value of the memories associated with these names are all dependent on the special impact any one of these events may have had on people. The greater the impact of the event, the more they will trigger associations and deep, meaningful memories.

Events in the life of Jesus can evoke strong associations in the minds of his followers. Some of them include the nativity, Gethsemane, the crucifixion, and the resurrection. The mere mention of one of these historic events in the life of Jesus can bring a flood of significant associations to the mind of the believer. Add "The Great Commission" to the list. Whenever you consider The Great Commission, let it stir within you greater and greater associations and an impulse to draw closer to God's will for your life.

Write out Matthew 28:18–20 on a piece of paper and carry it with you for a week. Memorize it. Meditate upon it. Know it. Learn to live it.

Let's consider God's commission (the Great Commission) under two headings: (1) authority and (2) authorization.

Authority

Jesus said that *all authority* had been given him—all authority in heaven and on earth. There is, and can be, no higher authority. Heaven and earth cover all known territory and everything in between. The more we understand the nature of his authority the more our confidence and faith in Christ will grow. This confidence will help us as we endeavor to live as a disciple.

Jesus' authority exists by virtue of his identity: God incarnate—God in the flesh. *"The word became flesh and dwelt among us"* (John 1:14). The reality of the supreme authority of Jesus is mentioned again and again.

- Authority over God's word: *"You have heard it said . . . but I say to you . . ."* (Matthew 5:21).

- Authority over nature:*" . . . even the wind and the waves obey him?"* (Matthew 8:27)

- Authority over sin: *"Who can forgive sins but God alone?"* (Mark 2:7)

- Authority over the Sabbath in Luke 6:5.

- Authority over all people as mentioned in John 17:2.

- Authority over all in the judgment in John 5:22.

- Authority over life and death in John 10:18 and Revelation 1:18.

When Jesus declared himself to be *"The Alpha and the Omega, the First and the Last, the Beginning and the End"* (Revelation 22:13), he was laying claim to his ultimate authority. No one lies outside the authority of Jesus Christ. He is the Beginning and the End of all things. All of creation will one day bow at the feet of Jesus:

At the name of Jesus every knee should bow, in heaven and on earth and under the earth . . . (Philippians 2:10).

Jesus has all authority because of who he is. He also has all authority because of what he has done. His life, death, burial, resurrection and ascension were events that broke the bondage of sin forever. Jesus descended from eternity and entered time. His glory was hidden as he went to the cross to ransom creation. He defeated death and the grave by the power of the resurrection.

God has raised this Jesus to life, and we are all witnesses of the fact. Exalted to the right hand of God . . . (Acts 2:32–33).

Jesus Christ is now *"seated at God's right hand"* (Colossians 3:1). This is a word picture for being in the position of absolute authority. This can be said of no one else. If Jesus has all authority in heaven and on earth and under the earth and he authorizes something, then his authorization should be given the highest consideration.

Authorization

After Jesus informed his disciples of his absolute authority, he immediately *authorized* them:

"Therefore, go . . ." Matthew 28:19

The "therefore" is there because Jesus just asserted the reality of his authority. We are sent on the basis of *his* authority. He himself has given us authorization. To be authorized means to be sanctioned and empowered. Jesus is much more committed to us than we will ever realize. We have been authorized to go in his name, that is, Jesus' authority. He went to a lot of trouble to make this authorization possible. Think of a door in a place of business with a sign fastened to it stating: "Authorized Personnel Only." Most people would not think of entering that door without authorization. However, the authorized person has every right and complete freedom to enter through the door. The disciple is such an authorized person.

The calling to discipleship that believers have received sets us apart from the rest of the world. Since the world at large has not received this commission, they do not have the same concerns we do. Discipleship with Christ is a privilege only for believers in Christ. It is our new mission. The definition of mission is "a task with a purpose." Our purpose for living and serving God should be clear for all believers. Our purpose in being disciples is to also go out and make disciples.

We cannot go out and make disciples if we ourselves are not committed to being disciples. Discipleship is a job that no one but those so authorized can fill: *"Go and make disciples of all people."* Who else is going to take this to heart but those who are committed to the purpose of God's mission?

We have a purpose, and we also have a task. We are to teach people to learn how to obey everything that Jesus has commanded. The implication of this is that we too will be learning obedience.

AUTHORITY ALERT

We live in an age where words like *authority* and *obedience* can strike horror into the hearts and minds of many people. This is nothing new. Our era is no different than any other era. It is human nature to rebel against authority.

C. S. Lewis wrote of his conversion to Christianity in a book entitled, *Surprised by Joy.* He conceded at the very end of the book that his main reason for avoiding belief in the gospel was the simple fact that he just wanted to be left alone. It is very instructive for us to consider that it was not for any deep intellectual or philosophical reason that Lewis resisted the gospel. It was simply that he wanted to be his own boss.

This is an ALERT to bring to light the fact that we need to *unlearn* as well as learn certain things. We need to *unlearn* natural ways of thinking and *learn* God's ways of thinking. We need to unlearn the idea that obedience is a negative word. We need to learn that obedience to God leads to blessing. Disciples are committed to learning how to obey in their everyday lives. We are to live lives of humble submission at the feet of Jesus.

We have been given authorization. We've been given purpose. We've been given a task. We have also been given a promise:

"Surely, I am with you always, to the very end of the age" (Matthew 28:20).

We might call this one of the hidden blessings of being a disciple. Remember, we are not in this alone. Jesus promised to be with us every step of the way. This communion with Jesus is a reality that can soften the scary prospects surrounding the call to obedience. It all melts into blessing in due time when Jesus is with us.

Believers have received God's commission to go out and impact the world. When do believers receive their commissions? We receive them the moment we are saved. The Holy Spirit has baptized us into the body of Christ (1 Corinthians 12:13). We have all the resources of heaven at our disposal and the very authorization of Jesus Christ himself. All this is a reflection of God's mission and his commission. This Great Commission now needs to be our commission. We are not alone. Jesus is in the mission along with us. Therefore, it is truly a co-mission.

Section Three

OUR COMMISSION

The Great Commission becomes our mission when we make a commitment of faith to yield to the Lordship of Jesus Christ. To be a disciple is to come under his discipline and training. I will highlight four components to discipleship.

1. Learning How to Obey

There are two misconceptions about discipleship. First, there is the mistaken idea that all Christians are disciples. There are many Christians who have not yielded to Christ. Many Christians have yet to give themselves fully to his leadership. Failure to yield to Jesus results in a faith that is weak. It also can lead to an unfruitful witness to the world. Second, there is also the mistaken idea that disciples are perfect. Disciples are not perfect. A disciple is a learner, and people who are learning will make mistakes; otherwise, they would have nothing to learn. A person who is a learner, by the very definition of the term, is expected to make mistakes.

Jesus has given us his divine invitation to learn:

Come to me, all you who are weary and burdened, and I will give you rest. Take my yoke upon you and learn from me, for I am gentle and humble in heart, and you will find rest for your souls. For my yoke is easy and my burden is light. (Matthew 11:28–30).

This is one of the grand invitations in the Bible. We can be "yoked" with Jesus: "Take my yoke upon you and learn from me." Jesus is the greatest, most patient of teachers. He also knows our hearts and things that we need far more than we do ourselves. His yoke is easy because it is worn in love and the burden is borne by him. It will require three things: that we be teachable, that we be committed, and that we have a willingness to be tested.

■ Teachable

The first step in learning something is to admit that we have a lot to learn. Have you ever tried to teach someone a skill but could not because of their attitude that they already knew what it was you were trying to teach them? This is called an unteachable attitude. God wants believers to be teachable—willing to learn. A humble attitude is required. We must come to the realization that our teacher knows more than we do.

Because most of us suffer from the ailment of not being very teachable, sometimes the Lord will use failure to get our attention. Failure can be a good teacher. Failure can be the two-by-four that God uses as a way to get through our mule-headedness. When David was king, he failed. After he learned his lesson, he composed one of the most beautiful and powerful poems of repentance in the Bible found in Psalm 51. Here is one verse:

The sacrifices of God are a broken spirit; a broken spirit and a contrite heart, O God, you will not despise (Psalm 51:17).

To be teachable requires that we are willing to repent. An attitude of repentance creates a climate of humility where instruction can take place with a willing heart and open ears. It is similar to that time in our teenage years when we were learning how to drive. We were placed in an ugly car with a huge sign that read, "Student Driver." It was an insult to our egos. We just couldn't wait to get out of that car and away from that humiliating sign and into our own cars where *we* would be the experts. Yet, we valued the goal so much that we gladly endured the "insult" of the sign. To be teachable is to be humble and willing to wear the sign, "Learner-disciple."

■ Committed

To be committed is to have new priorities. Commitment requires perseverance. We must have a commitment that will stand up against hard times, bad moods, unscheduled setbacks, and even gross failure. Paul described commitment this way:

Not that I have already obtained all this, or have already been made perfect, but I press on to take hold of that for which Christ Jesus took hold of me. Brothers, I do not consider myself yet to have taken hold of it. But one thing I do: Forgetting what is behind and straining toward what is ahead, I press on toward the goal to win the prize for which God has called me heavenward in Christ Jesus (Philippians 3:12–14).

Three times Paul admitted that he had not yet arrived. Failure and setbacks would not stop him. His eye was on the goal, and he was determined to press on toward Christ. We need to have a tenacious grip on this kind of commitment if we are to be disciple-learners in the kingdom of God, because there is much to distract us and knock us off course.

There are times we will have to commit and then commit again. This may seem humbling at times because people may be ashamed to admit that they have failed. We might even have to recommit every day. The point is to be like Paul: *"This one thing I do: Forgetting what is behind and straining toward what is ahead . . ."* Never give up.

■ Tested

One of the biggest surprises that hits all believers, especially when they commit to discipleship, is that there will come times of testing. Faith will be put to the test:

Dear friends, do not be surprised at the painful trial you are suffering, as though something strange were happening to you (1 Peter 4:12).

If anyone would come after me, he must deny himself and take up his cross and follow me (Mark 8:34).

There will be times of testing that will require us to choose whom we will follow. Will we follow the Lord in the situation, or will we follow our own desires? It is not always as simple as it might seem. The choice of whom we will serve, self or Christ, can be very subtle until we come to understand exactly where the tension lies. It usually lies where our own will crosses the will of God. At these times we are forced to make a choice. Many times we won't easily recognize God's will at first because we may have spent most of our lives with little concern for it. The issue of the will of God must be addressed in every area of our lives. This causes tension and conflict.

There could be a conflict in a relationship with another person. We might have an attitude that God would have us work to change. Whatever the situation, we will often find ourselves confronted with the challenge of having to make a choice. We will have to choose between God's will and ours. Our old ways of doing things will no longer be acceptable. The process of making this choice will be a time of testing for us. Sometimes making a choice may be the most spiritual thing we will ever do.

Remember the yoke that Jesus spoke about? He will give it a yank, and we'll realize we need to move in a new direction. We can no longer move about in a self-centered, carefree manner. We are now careful as we move through life, keeping God's will as our central focus. Choosing God's will may cause some pain, but a disciple is willing to go through these times of trials and tests. This is our training. We will learn by the help of God. Sometime this training will happen in the midst of pain and disappointment. Eventually, our trial will be over. We will then look back on our times of testing with gratitude when we see the fruit that God has produced in our lives.

2. Becoming Equipped

As we enter into the realm of learning how to obey, we will also need to start the process of becoming equipped. This means our training will take us to new levels of usefulness in the kingdom of God. We will become useful vessels in the hands of God to impact the world around us. We have looked at Ephesians 4 in the chapter on the church. Let's take a deeper look:

It was he who gave some to be apostles, some to be prophets, some to be evangelists, and some to be pastors and teachers, to prepare God's people for works of service, so that the body of Christ may be built up until we all reach unity in the faith and in the knowledge of the Son of God and become mature, attaining to the whole measure of the fullness of Christ.

Then we will no longer be infants, tossed back and forth by the waves, and blown here and there by every wind of teaching and by the cunning and craftiness of men in their deceitful scheming. Instead, speaking the truth in love, we will in all things grow up into him who is the Head, that is, Christ. From him the whole body, joined and held together by every supporting ligament, grows and builds itself up in love, as each part does its work (Ephesians 4:11–16).

The idea of becoming equipped is illustrated by the image of fishing nets being pulled on to the shore. There they are mended. Once mended, they are then put back into service. This is the same for the believer. We have, in a sense, been pulled from the world, and God has begun to mend us. We are to yield ourselves to the process of becoming equipped. Just as fishermen will use their mended nets, God will also use us. In a lot of ways the church is a hospital, a body and fender shop, a university, a reclamation center, an army barracks, and a training depot. We are in the process of being prepared with an eye toward productive service for the kingdom of God.

The goal is both a combination of maturity and of usefulness. There is no unemployment in the kingdom of God. Everyone can employ their gifts in an endless variety of ways. Disciples who are committed to becoming equipped will find it exciting to come to church and serve with their gifts and talents. They will be compelled to get involved. They will find it meaningless to live a secular life. They will serve God every day. Their lives will be a reflection of God's equipping power, all to his glory. They will discover it as the most exciting and adventurous way to live.

3. Being Fruitful

Learning how to obey and becoming equipped all take place in the context of relationship. Becoming equipped for use in the kingdom of God is a rich and meaningful pursuit. We are intimately in contact with Jesus in such a way that will bear fruit.

I am the true vine, and my Father is the gardener. He cuts off every branch in me that bears no fruit, while every branch that does bear fruit he prunes so that it will be even more fruitful. You are already clean because of the word I have spoken to you. Remain in me, and I will remain in you. No branch can bear fruit by itself; it must remain in the vine. Neither can you bear fruit unless you remain in me.

I am the vine; you are the branches. If a man remains in me and I in him, he will bear much fruit; apart from me you can do nothing. If anyone does not remain in me, he is like a branch that is thrown away and withers; such branches are picked up, thrown into the fire and burned. If you remain in me and my words remain in you, ask whatever you wish, and it will be given you. This is to my Father's glory, that you bear much fruit, showing yourselves to be my disciple (John 15:1–8).

We must be in close communion with Jesus. This involves a life of learning how to depend on him. We must be willing to give up our old life of independence and replace it with one of dependence. This is not often as easy or as simple as it sounds. It goes completely against human nature. It is something that will have to be learned because we have spent a lifetime fighting for our independence. We can more easily see ourselves signing a declaration of independence than bowing at the foot of the cross to sign a declaration of dependence. A disciple is called to learn to be dependent and to learn to live a life of trust. As Isaiah 55:8 says, *"God's ways are not our ways."*

In order to learn God's ways we will be subjected to his pruning process. This is an apt metaphor. Just as a tree must be pruned of its old wood so it can bear more fruit, we too must be pruned of our old ways so that we can bear fruit for God. This may involve pain and loss of ease, but God also will bring special comfort as well. God will see that our lives will bear fruit for him as we grow in our relationship with him.

There are many kinds of fruit. There is the fruit of the Spirit:

The fruit of the Spirit is love, joy, peace, patience, kindness, goodness, faithfulness, gentleness and self-control (Galatians 5:22–23).

Look over these nine traits. They reflect the results of a life dedicated to being trained and *pruned* by the hand of God. Think of the revolutionary effect these character traits would have on our lives and on the lives of those around us.

There is the fruit that comes from working among people with the goal of leading them to the Lord:

When he saw the crowds, he had compassion on them, because they were harassed and helpless, like sheep without a shepherd. Then he said to his disciples, "The harvest is plentiful but the workers are few. Ask the Lord of the harvest, therefore, to send out workers into his harvest field" (Matthew 9:36–38).

One of the greatest blessings of bearing fruit for the kingdom of God is allowing our lives to be used in bringing people to the Lord. Who else is Jesus going to turn to except to his very own disciples? There are many examples of fruit and fruitfulness, but one thing is certain—it is to God's glory that we bear much fruit showing ourselves to be his disciples.

4. Enjoying Privilege

The commitment to discipleship leads to a surprising life of privilege. It might not be privilege in the way the world thinks of privilege. It is the privilege of involvement and sharing in ministry with the Lord. It is an ever-deepening relationship unknown to those outside the kingdom of God. Jesus told a parable about a man who went away on a long journey. Upon leaving he entrusted his property to his servants:

To one he gave five talents of money, and to another two talents, and to another one talent, each according to his ability. Then he went on his journey (Matthew 25:14–15).

When the man returned from his journey he rewarded the servants who gained and multiplied what was entrusted to them:

Well done good and faithful servant! You have been faithful in little things; I will put you in charge of many things. Come and share in your master's happiness! (Matthew 25:21)

To serve was a privilege and it led to more privilege. Faithfulness in little things led to greater things. We cannot calculate the hidden blessings derived from our small gestures of faithfulness in fulfilling the calling that the Lord has on our lives. Notice that it also led to the added blessing of deeper fellowship and mutual enjoyment between the servant and the master: *"Come and share in your master's happiness."*

CONCLUSION

It is amazing where discipleship will take a person. It will lead to some fantastic blessings. Think of some of the people in the Bible that God called: Abraham, Sarah, Moses, Joshua, Gideon, Deborah, David, Esther, Isaiah, and Jeremiah. Jesus called Mary, Matthew, Peter, James, John, Lydia, Paul, Lois, Eunice, and Timothy to ministry. We may not rise to their levels, but we do have one thing in common with them. They, like us, had to start from the very beginning. None of them were born into greatness. It came to them as they followed the leading of the Lord. None of them had any idea where God would lead them, or what a blessed life they would lead. They all had to start from the beginning (or a new beginning) just like you and me.

The one missing ingredient in the lives of many Christians is that they honestly have not yet begun to take the call of discipleship seriously. How many Matthews, Johns, Peters and Lydias are out there waiting to blossom? *"It is to my Father's glory that you bear much fruit showing yourselves to be my disciples"* (John 15:8).

STUDY QUESTIONS

1. Can you list three or four examples from the Old Testament that demonstrate God's mission of redemption?

2. Can you list three or four examples from the New Testament that demonstrate the same mission?

3. Can you commit to memory The Great Commission passage in Matthew 28:18–20?

4. How would you explain to someone the nature of the authority that Jesus has and how it relates to his giving The Great Commission?

5. How does his authorization affect those believers who have committed themselves to be in discipleship with him?

6. How do you think Jesus' personal promise at the very end of the great commission will affect you as you follow him?

7. What are the four components that are involved in our living out a life of discipleship as discussed in the section: "Our Mission?"
   Hint: *(learning, becoming, being, enjoying)*

8. Can you give a brief summary of each component?

9. How might you pray to the Lord for help in being committed to discipleship right now?

QUESTIONS PEOPLE ASK

■ *If people claim to be Christians, but haven't made Jesus "Lord," does that prove they are not saved?*

This is sometimes called the "Lordship" debate. Some people would say that if believers are not exhibiting exemplary Christian behavior, then they have not made Jesus their Lord. One side of the debate would say that the failure to make Jesus their Lord, by definition, makes them not saved. The problem arises when it comes time to make the necessary judgments as to who is, or who is not, saved based on observable behavior. First of all, who will judge? Second, when will a person be judged as being "not saved?" For all we know that particular person might be in the very midst of the crucible of learning. Nobody really knows except the Lord himself.

There were times when all of us would have been hard pressed to determine the status of either Peter or Judas while they were walking with Jesus. There were times when Judas looked as if he was a great disciple. He even sat at the Lord's right hand during the Last Supper. Peter, on the other hand, often looked the part of a failure, even to the point of denying the Lord. This should serve as an example for us just how hard it is to make such determinations based on outward appearances.

Once we leave room for the grace of God and the confession of believers themselves, it is true that with birth, growth follows. Believers who are not growing in their relationship with the Lord are missing the fullness and richness that awaits them. Our calling is to bring encouragement and exhortation that would lead them to desire growth.

The apostle Peter gave a beautiful teaching on Christian growth and maturity (2 Peter 1:3–9) concluding with the following exhortation:

Therefore, my brothers, be all the more eager to make your calling and election sure. For if you do these things you will never fall, and you will receive a rich welcome into the eternal kingdom of our Lord and Savior Jesus Christ (2 Peter 1:10–11).

A life of committed (eager) discipleship/training will do wonders in helping to make any believer's "calling and election sure."

■ *What about failure? How many times can I fail and still be a disciple?*

We will always fail. We will always fall short in some way. We may grow to the degree that it seems that we sin much less in both thought and deed. However, the true issue is not sinless perfection (which is impossible), but repentance.

Repentance is a beautiful gift from God. It is the mark of true freedom. We are free to admit our mistakes and shortcomings. We do not have to hide them. If we allow the unrealistic pressure to be perfect to keep us from being able to admit our faults, we will find ourselves in bondage and our hearts will be hardened. We will also find ourselves living like hypocrites. It might take some getting used to, but repentance *must* become a lifestyle for a disciple. One way of thinking about this is what is called "walking in the light."

God is light; in him there is no darkness at all. If we claim to have fellowship with him yet walk in the darkness, we lie and do not live by the truth. But if we walk in the light, as he is in the light, we have fellowship with one another, and the blood of Jesus, his Son, purifies us from all sin.

If we claim to be without sin, we deceive ourselves and the truth is not in us. If we confess our sins, he is faithful and just and will forgive us our sins and purify us from all unrighteousness If we claim we have not sinned, we make him out to be a liar and his word has no place in our lives (1 John 1:5–10).

Part of walking in the light is to keep short accounts with God and with people. The longer we wait—the more we procrastinate—the more we postpone healing and growth. Be willing to repent. Be willing to walk in the light. It is not about failure or success, but about truth, honesty, and keeping our hearts soft before the Lord and with those around us.

Chapter Eight

PRAYER

KEY POINTS

- The concept of the priesthood of the believer
- How to overcome hindrances to prayer
- How to develop a healthy prayer life

We know that Jesus spent whole nights alone in prayer. He prayed publicly. He prayed privately. At times, he prayed out loud so those around him could overhear. Jesus taught on the topic of prayer, and he devoted several parables to the subject of prayer. He even gave us a model on which to base our prayers. Jesus expected his disciples to pray. Prayer is an absolutely indispensable necessity in the lives of all those who follow Jesus. Prayer is one way we communicate with God.

As you study this section you will find new confidence and a renewed sense of calling to prayer like never before. We will begin by looking at one of Jesus' parables on prayer and focus on three areas: (1) the reason for prayer, (2) overcoming hindrances to prayer, and (3) practicing prayer.

Section One

A PARABLE ON PRAYER

Then Jesus told his disciples a parable to show them that they should always pray and not give up. He said: "In a certain town there was a judge who neither feared God nor cared about men. And there was a widow in that town who kept coming to him with the plea, 'Grant me justice against my adversary.'

"For some time he refused. But finally he said to himself, 'Even though I don't fear God or care about men, yet because this widow keeps bothering me, I will see that she gets justice, so that she won't eventually wear me out with her coming!'"

And the Lord said, "Listen to what the unjust judge says. And will not God bring about justice for his chosen ones who cry out to him day and night? Will he keep putting them off? I tell you, he will see that they get justice, and quickly. However, when the Son of Man comes, will he find faith on earth?" (Luke 18:1–8).

Parables are a genre of literature that are found in both the Old and New Testaments. Jesus was the expert in the art of the parable. A parable is a story. It is a teaching tool. A parable has a way of sticking like Velcro to our hearts and minds. The truth of a parable can penetrate quickly to those willing to listen or it can slowly seep into the minds of those who are not so willing. Truth, in the form of a story, can be a kind of friendly persuasion.

We are fortunate that Jesus gave us this parable. Jesus so graciously reached out to us by parables. He did this because he loves us and wants to get his truth into our lives. What a beautiful and loving way to lead us into his truth! Parables were a great learner-friendly means of teaching. We are also told right up front the major purpose of this parable was to show us that we should always pray and not give up.

Jesus knows human nature. It takes faith to pray. He knows that we are subject to discouragement. He knows that we can be flattened by our circumstances and that this can flatten our faith. Our faith will be strengthened as we are informed about prayer and the view Jesus had regarding it. We will now look at the reason behind prayer. I hope these reasons will lead you to a deeper life of prayer.

Section Two

THE REASON FOR PRAYER

1. Calling

We are people who belong to the Lord. It has always been God's plan to have a people who would represent him on earth:

Now if you obey me fully and keep my covenant, then out of all nations you will be my treasured possession. Although the whole earth is mine, you will be for me a kingdom of priests and a holy nation . . . (Exodus 19:5–6).

The Apostle Peter, referring to Christians, showed how this calling was fulfilled in the gospel:

But you are a chosen people, a royal priesthood, a holy nation, a people belonging to God, that you may declare the praises of him who called you out of darkness into his wonderful light. Once you were not a people, but now you are the people of God; once you had not received mercy, but now you have received mercy (1 Peter 2:9–10).

There are two sides to this "holy priesthood." The first is the fact that we are priests. This is all due to the work of Christ on the cross. We, who have placed our faith in him, now have complete access to God through Christ. Therefore, every born-again believer is a priest in the truest sense of the term. The second side to this priesthood is the fact that it is a "holy" priesthood. We belong to God as the "people of God." We are separated unto God. We are called out of the world and set apart (holy) unto God.

There is a common expression, "the priesthood of the believer." It is the divine calling of every believer. There are no exceptions. It is our calling because it is who we are, and who God made us to be, through the work of Christ. It is our calling to pray.

2. Duty

Since God has called us out of the world and made us his people, we now have the God-ordained duty to pray. The definition of duty is this: "a task or function arising out of position." It is a logical association that makes sense. The following examples will show how this definition of duty works.

If you were to witness a crime, you would naturally go to a law enforcement officer. You wouldn't go to your neighbor and ask him to pursue the criminal. It is not his duty. Yet, it is perfectly acceptable and natural to go to the one who has been given the duty to go after criminals. If you were in a clothing store and you were looking for that perfect shirt to match the rest of your outfit, whom would you ask for help? Of course, you would ask the sales clerk. If you flagged down another customer and told him that you needed help finding a certain item, he'd probably give you a funny look. It is not his duty to help you.

During WWII, General Eisenhower came to the center of the staging area for the launching of the D-Day invasion. He spoke to the troops and said, "Don't look for anyone else to do your job. It's all up to you." Eisenhower's challenge was a good illustration of a task or function arising out of position. This is the very definition of duty.

We have a task and purpose arising out of our position as people who belong to God. God looks for no one other than his people to fulfill the duty of prayer.

3. Privilege

Only those who belong to God through Jesus Christ have the privileged status of being able to "move the hands of God" through prayer. This is not to say that God does not hear if anyone else should happen to pray, but that we have the God-given right to pray. We also hold dear the many promises of God that he will hear our prayers. The door of privilege has been opened to us. We have been given access into the heavenly realms. It is our gain if we accept this privilege. God's power is advanced by our prayers for those in need of our intercession.

There are stories of people who have lived lives of poverty. Upon their death, their affairs were put in order and it was discovered that they had been hording a million dollars under a mattress or somewhere in the walls of their dwelling. The world stands amazed that people would have such potential right at their fingertips, yet all the while choose to live the life of the underprivileged. That may be their choice, but we have been given the privilege of prayer and are called to put it into practice.

There may come a day when we might be allowed to see the secret, inner workings behind the scenes in the kingdom of God. How many answers to prayer will be seen due to prayers that we ourselves have offered in faith? Prayer is a wonderful privilege given to believers with the potential to reach into eternity.

Believers are a privileged people. We have God for us, along with Jesus. We have been given the gift of the Holy Spirit. The angels of heaven are ministering spirits on our behalf. We have the word of God filled with great and precious promises. We have great churches and teachers everywhere. We have the fellowship of all our fellow believers as well. We also have thousands of years of answers to prayers as our heritage, not to mention the answered prayers that we have already experienced in our lives.

The Apostle Paul gave us a glimpse into the privileges of being a believer. In his letter to the Ephesians, he fills the first three chapters outlining our incredible privileges. Among other things, he offered this prayer:

I keep asking that the God of our Lord Jesus Christ, the glorious Father, may give you the Spirit of wisdom and revelation, so that you may know him better. I pray also that the eyes of your heart may be enlightened in order that you may know the hope to which he has called you, the riches of his glorious inheritance in the saints (Ephesians 1:17–18).

The first three chapters of Ephesians is a portion of Scripture that all believers should study. Paul concluded the end of chapter three with another prayer, and here is how he ended that prayer:

Now to him who is able to do immeasurably more than all we ask or imagine, according to his power that is at work within us, to him be glory in the church and in Christ Jesus throughout all generations, forever and ever! Amen (Ephesians 3:20–21).

This prayer is still alive today. There have been answers to prayers ever since the first human being walked on the earth. It is a gift for all believers down through the centuries. It has lost none of its power. Yes, we are privileged people and it is our privilege to pray.

4. Need

We are pilgrims on an earthly sojourn. We do not belong to the kingdom of this world, but to the kingdom of God. Our citizenship is in heaven. We are aliens and foreigners on earth. This is something we should never forget. Once we come to God through Jesus Christ, we are taken out of the world. As a result, we will always have special need of help. Jesus said:

If the world hates you, keep in mind that it hated me first. If you belonged to the world, it would love you as its own. As it is, you do not belong to the world, but I have chosen you out of the world. That is why the world hates you" (John 15:18–19).

Later, Jesus would say, *"I have told you these things, so that you would have peace. In the world you will have trouble. But take heart! I have overcome the world"* (John 16:33).

We need to pray because we cannot count on the help and resources of this world since we do not claim earth as our home. We must depend on heaven's help.

We also need to pray because we live in a fallen world. Sometimes, even with our greatest efforts and noblest intentions, the ground will still produce for us "thorns and thistles" (Genesis 3:18). It's part of the curse of the fall. We need help to counteract the effects of this fallen world.

Another reason we need to pray is that we are fallen creatures ourselves. Yes, we have been given a new nature in Christ, but our old, fallen nature is still with us. This is all the more reason to pray.

To help illustrate our need to pray, let's take a look at the way Jesus prayed:

Very early in the morning, while it was still dark, Jesus got up, left the house and went off to a solitary place where he prayed (Mark 1:35).

Jesus often withdrew to lonely places and prayed (Luke 5:16).

Jesus went out to a mountainside to pray and spent the night praying to God (Luke 6:12).

The implication should be obvious. If Jesus, who was the perfect, sinless, holy, Son of God needed to pray, how about you and me?

There is something mysterious about prayer. We all seem to know that we need to partake in it, but often find ourselves somehow falling short. In a TV interview Billy Graham was asked if there was anything that he regretted in his long and illustrious career. He answered quickly, "My only regret is that I have not spent more time in prayer." Even a man such as this, still felt an overwhelming sense of having fallen short in his calling to pray. He was sensitive to the necessity of prayer.

Jesus said, *"Apart from me you can do nothing"* (John 15:5). To not pray is to presume that we can operate as aliens in this fallen world without the help of heaven. This is a presumption we cannot live with. Have you ever thought of praying, but found that you just were not in the mood, or couldn't pray because you were hounded by a nagging sense of failure? Think of it this way—we must pray simply because we need to pray. The fact that we *need* to pray is reason enough to pray.

5. Relationship

We were created for relationship with God. Prayer is a great way to celebrate and enjoy this relationship. We can pray while driving our car or while at the kitchen sink washing the dishes. We can pray while walking down the road or while we are at work. Prayer is communication and communion with God. It should be a natural part of our relationship with him.

We can also pray using the Psalms or other Scriptures. The following are some examples from the Psalms that touch the deepest part of our hearts:

O LORD, how many are my foes! How many rise up against me! Many are saying of me, "God will not deliver him." But you are a shield around me, O LORD; you bestow glory on me and lift up my head" (Psalm 3:1–3).

As the deer pants for streams of water, so my soul pants for you, O God. My soul thirsts for God, for the living God. When can I go and meet with God? (Psalm 42:1–2)

Search me, O God, and know my heart; test me and know my anxious thoughts. See if there is any wicked way in me, and lead me in the way everlasting (Psalm 139:23–24).

I cry aloud to the LORD; I lift up my voice to the LORD for mercy. I pour out my complaint before him; before him I tell my trouble (Psalm 142:1–2).

These are small examples of the many Psalms that we can use in our own prayers to help capture the passion deep within our hearts. The Psalms also help to give us direction in our prayers. The Bible is a great prayer book. It can be used to deepen our relationship with the Lord as we use the Scriptures in prayers.

We can also pray as we worship. The many hymns and choruses we sing can be sung with renewed fervency as we realize we are actually singing our prayer. We are communicating and communing with our Lord as we worship.

TIME OUT

Take time to review the five reasons for prayer that have been discussed. The headings were CALLING, DUTY, PRIVILEGE, NEED, and RELATIONSHIP. Go over each one slowly. Reflect on how these reasons have relevance in your life. Let each one energize your own prayer life. Maybe one may stand out more than others.

Write out each of the five reasons for prayer on a piece of paper and see how many Scriptural examples you can give under each heading. Add your own thoughts and meditations under each heading.

Set aside some time for prayer. Ask the Lord for help in making prayer a new priority for you.

Section Three

OVERCOMING HINDRANCES TO PRAYER

In this section three hindrances to prayer will be presented. Hopefully, at the conclusion of this section, any hindrances to prayer that may have plagued you will evaporate as your faith becomes sharpened.

There are three problems we all face that make prayer difficult. The three problems are (1) sin, (2) unbelief, and (3) ignorance.

1. Sin

It is no accident that guilt and shame cause us to withdraw from fellowship with God. Since prayer is fellowship with God, it only takes the least bit of guilt or shame to cause us to withdraw from fellowship. This is especially true as we draw closer to God. We will be even more sensitized to our own sin and shortcomings. Notice the first word in the following verse:

If we confess our sins, he is faithful and just and will forgive us our sins and purify us from all unrighteousness (1 John 1:9).

"If" is the operative word in 1 John 1:9. It is the difference between this promise being fulfilled or the promise remaining empty. Confession has been defined as telling God what he already knows about us. We need to unburden ourselves and be open and honest with God. Confession is the doorway to continual fellowship with God. God promises to be faithful. He will always forgive. He will be faithful in his promises. That is his nature. God's love and faithfulness will never end. He will always do what he promises:

Your love, O LORD, reaches to the heavens, your faithfulness to the skies (Psalm 36:5).

God is faithful. He is also just. The just price was paid at the cross. We have powerful and complete forgiveness if we sincerely confess our sins. The Son of God paid the full price. Think about the guilt and shame that might keep us from praying. How long should we grovel? Would one day suffice? How about a month? Why not go all out and crawl on our knees to a shrine as an act of penance? The reasonable and Scriptural solution is confession and then to trust God to honor his word. Anything other than this might lead to the mistaken idea that we can somehow merit forgiveness. Since we can merit nothing, what option is there but to confess? Yes, we may sin, but let's not let it keep us from approaching God. Learn to obey 1 John 1:9 by living on the obedient side of the "if."

2. Unbelief

Prayer can be difficult. Prayer requires faith. Lack of faith can be a hindrance to prayer. Believers can go months, even years, without much praying simply because they have not had their faith ignited in such a way that would make prayer a priority.

One day Jesus' disciples made this request of him, *"Lord, teach us to pray"* (Luke 11:1). The disciples had seen some amazing things while they traveled with Jesus. They saw more than 5,000 people fed with a few loaves and fishes. They saw the lame walk and the blind see. People were raised from the dead. The one thing they would ask to be taught had nothing to do with these spectacular miracles. It had to do with something much less spectacular. It had to do with prayer.

Perhaps they simply wanted a model prayer to repeat like other teachers gave to their followers. Or it could have been that they saw Jesus in prayer. They noticed that it was a priority for him. Jesus prayed with the intensity of really being in communication with God. This was something foreign to them. Perhaps in their struggle prayer had become a bland, lifeless ritual devoid of meaning. Or perhaps they seldom prayed at all. "Jesus, we've seen *you* pray. Please teach us to pray."

A man wrote a letter to the editor of a newspaper saying, "Praying is procrastinating, delaying the inevitable. No one ever answered any prayer, nor ever will. Praying is no more than talking to oneself. A thinking person plans and works things out. A non-thinking person prays."

The man who wrote this letter obviously had no faith to pray. Since faith is a requirement for prayer, it is important to realize that faith doesn't always come easy. Many people struggle with prayer. It is a difficult task. Discouragement can cause a person's prayer life to become stagnant and eventually die out. The writer of the book of Hebrews wrote a message about faith:

Without faith it is impossible to please God, because anyone who comes to him must believe that he exists and that he rewards those who earnestly seek him (Hebrews 11:6).

Faith is essential to prayer. The subject of prayer may be overwhelming to us or we may have doubt that a problem will ever be solved. These are the times when our faith may be tested. When we find that we have to work at prayer is when we must put our faith to work. Sometimes prayer is work, but because it may be work does not mean that we don't have faith. The fact that prayer can be work is all the more reason to pray to exercise our faith. Eventually the battle will be won if we refuse to give up. Remember, it takes faith to pray.

3. Ignorance

Ignorance can be a hindrance to prayer simply because we might not know God's will. Knowing God's Word will strengthen our faith. One of the purposes of God's Word is to cause our faith to increase. We will find that God is often more willing to answer our prayers than we are to pray. There are numerous invitations to approach God in prayer written in the Bible:

Ask and it will be given to you; seek and you will find; knock and the door will be opened to you. For everyone who asks receives; he who seeks finds; and to him who knocks, the door will be opened (Matthew 7:7–8).

Therefore, since we have such a great high priest who has gone through the heavens, Jesus the Son of God, let us hold firmly to the faith we profess. For we do not have a high priest who is unable to sympathize with our weaknesses, but we have one who has been tempted in every way, just as we are—yet without sin. Let us then approach the throne of grace with confidence, so that we may receive mercy and find grace to help us in our time of need (Hebrews 4:14–16).

APPROACH ALERT

Sometimes our emotions or personal circumstances can keep us from approaching the Lord in prayer. We might be overcome by feelings of dread or doubt. It could be our fault or nobody's fault, but the feelings might be there just the same. We find that we simply cannot or will not approach the Lord in prayer while this inner struggle is going on. Spend time meditating on the great invitation to prayer written in Hebrews 4:14–16.

Notice how strongly we are encouraged to approach God. Jesus is our very own high priest who is sitting at God's right hand and is, in fact, the Son of God! Because he became a human being, he is able to sympathize with our weaknesses. We are exhorted to approach with confident boldness. We are not to allow feelings of doubt and inadequacy to keep us away. Even though we might very well be full of doubts, our doubts are not the issue. The issue is to approach the throne of grace.

A throne is a seat of power and authority. Think of all the many unapproachable thrones that exist on this planet. Almost all seats of authority on earth are designed to keep people away, especially those who are weak and in need. Try having a personal audience with the CEO of a large corporation. Or try having access to a sultan or a prince. How about a visit with the President of the United States? None of these meetings will happen because these are unapproachable thrones.

Here, however, we have a throne that is above all other thrones. The throne of God is designed to draw us near, not keep us away. What will we find when we approach God's seat of authority? We will *"receive mercy and find grace to help us in our time of need."* Mercy implies receiving a gift when we do not deserve it. Grace is the channel that moves the power of mercy. When do we receive this help? We are promised help *"in our time of need."* Many people are the most fearful of approaching God in their time of need. Yet this is just the time we are told to approach. If we wait until we have no need, then we will have defeated the purpose for coming to God in the first place.

This is an ALERT to encourage all believers to do as God's Word instructs. We all will be forced to choose between obedience to feelings and emotions or obedience to God's Word. Choose God's Word and pray with faith.

Let's take another look at the parable from Luke 18. The judge in the parable neither feared God nor cared about men. On the scale of human kindness, he would be on the lowest level. In fact, Jesus labeled him an "unjust judge." The woman in the parable was a widow. Widows were among the weakest and most vulnerable people in that society. Therefore, Jesus cast the parable with two characters that were a study of contrasts: the judge, the strongest and one who wields the most power, and the widow, the weakest and one who had no power.

As we contrast the unjust judge to God, we will see the point that Jesus was trying to make:

- To the judge, the widow was a stranger. We are no strangers to God. He knows us better than we know ourselves.

- The judge kept turning the widow away. God never turns us away. He bids us to come and to come with bold confidence.

- The widow came to an unjust judge. We come to a God who is just. He is, in fact, The Righteous Judge.

- The widow was given no encouragement to approach the judge for help. We are given every encouragement to come. In fact, we are chastised for NOT approaching.

- The widow could only come to see the judge at certain times. God keeps no office hours. He never slumbers or sleeps.

- The widow's urgent need provokes the unjust judge to anger. God welcomes our need. In fact, he will often move heaven and earth just to show us how needy we truly are.

- The widow had no one to serve as her advocate. We have been given an advocate of unimaginable magnitude. *"If God be for us, who can be against us . . . Christ Jesus is at the right hand of God and is also interceding for us . . . the Holy Spirit himself intercedes for us"* (Romans 8:26, 31, 34).

If the widow could receive justice at the hand of an unjust judge, how much more will we receive the help we need as we come to the judge of all righteousness who loves us with an undying love? His love for us was proven on the cross. The main point of the parable is that we should *"always pray and not give up"* (Luke 18:1). In the light of so much encouragement, how could we do otherwise?

Ignorance of the will of God regarding prayer can actually hinder our praying. When we come to know how much God desires for us to exercise our right and privilege of prayer, the more likely we will take advantage of this God-given, God-ordained spiritual blessing.

Section Four

PRACTICING PRAYER

One of the secrets to prayer is that we learn by doing. When the disciples asked Jesus to teach them to pray, he responded by giving them a model prayer. This model prayer has become known as the Lord's Prayer. While it is rightly known as the Lord's Prayer, it can actually be called "The Disciples' Prayer." It was given as a model to follow. We do not have to follow rote prayers, but we can benefit from guidance. There is no better guide in the practice of prayer than Jesus.

The Lord's model prayer (Matthew 6:9–13) is reproduced below. It is broken down into categories to help you to see the outline of this magnificent aid to prayer.

PRAISE AND ADORATION

"Our Father in heaven, hallowed be your name."

The prayer begins by spending time praising and thanking God for his goodness and love. We don't want to barge in to the King's chamber by rudely blurting out demands. We benefit when we exercise proper decorum and respect. Entering into the presence of God with praise and thanksgiving will teach us awe and reverence. It will help us remember his greatness. This will benefit us as much as any answered prayer we might receive.

Example: "Thank you Father for your goodness to me. Your grace is precious. You have been my Shepherd and Savior. I thank and praise you . . .."

INTERCESSION

"Your kingdom come, your will be done on earth as it is done in heaven."

God's will is executed perfectly in heaven, but this fallen world is still a work in progress. We are waiting for final redemption. However, the will of God can be manifested in answer to prayer. His will is being done to a large extent in the lives of those who belong to him, but there are many places God's will is not being done. This is the part of the prayer where we can intercede for God's will to be done in the lives of others, in our own lives, and for all the needs around us.

Example: "Dear Lord, let your will be done in Pete's life. He needs help in finding a job. Lord, I also pray that you would look after my sister who is ill . . .."

PETITION

"Give us this day our daily bread."

Daily bread can stand to mean any need that we might have. After we have properly entered into communication and have made intercession for others, we can now bring our petitions before the Lord. He has instructed us to do so. He is our source. We are to lay out all of our needs and concerns before him.

Example: "Help me to provide for my family. Please look after my new position at work and give me favor with my new boss . . .."

CONFESSION

"Forgive us our debts, as we have also forgiven our debtors."

Our willingness to forgive others is linked with our having been forgiven ourselves. The two cannot be separated. So strongly are they linked, that it is assumed we have forgiven others before we would presume to ask God for the same. This will cause us to walk circumspectly, not leaving broken relationships behind us. Therefore, the door is open to enjoy unbroken communion with God as we strive to repair any broken relationships we might have with others.

Example: "Dear God, have mercy on me a sinner. Help me to grow stronger in my walk with you. Please forgive me for _____. . . . . And, Lord, please help me to forgive _____ for _____."

GUIDANCE AND PROTECTION

"And lead us not into temptation, but deliver us from the evil one."

Our prayer ends with the request for God's leading in our lives. God has promised to guide our steps as we depend on him. We need to live a life of humble dependence. We also live in a fallen world that is under the influence of "the evil one." Prayer is needed to steer us away from Satan's influences and the influences of this fallen world.

Example: "Let your hand be upon me today as I am at work. Keep my thoughts set on you, O Lord. Guide me in my decisions . . . .

PRAISE AND ADORATION

"For yours is the kingdom and the power and the glory for-ever. Amen."

This last line is not in the earliest manuscripts, but it is found in later ones. Just as we don't want to abruptly enter the King's chamber without a proper entrance, we should not slam the door on our way out. It is good to end our prayers with praise and thanksgiving.

Example: "Thank you, Lord, for all your love and care. I praise you for your faithfulness . . . .

This is the model prayer that Jesus gave that may serve as a template for an extended time in communion with God. Not all prayer need follow this pattern because not all prayer is as formal as this. Many times our praying may be spontaneous and perhaps not as comprehensive. However, this is the model Jesus gave that can help us to cultivate a life of prayer. The more we use this pattern, the more it will become second nature to us.

TIME OUT

Write out the outline headings and the verses from the Lord's Prayer. Make your own personal prayer chart using the categories taken from the Lord's Prayer. Now, find a quiet place where you can be alone and begin praying according to the outline. Pray every day for a month using this outline.

We learn by doing. The rewards are infinite. God is infinite. Remember the infinite promise given at the end of chapter three of Ephesians?

Now to him who is able to do immeasurably more than all we ask or imagine, according to his power that is at work within us (Ephesians 3:20).

CONCLUSION

The parable in Luke 18 began with this introduction: *"Then Jesus told his disciples a parable to show them that they should always pray and not give up."* After the parable there is this interesting and arresting comment by Jesus: *"However, when the Son of Man comes, will he find faith on earth?"* The implication could be that the trials and perils of life of a believer are such that it could render a person faithless. Prayer, among other things relating to our faith, may fall victim to the daily discouragements and trials of life. The question remains, who will fall off and who will continue to pursue a vibrant and rewarding life of prayer with the Lord in the midst of it all?

STUDY QUESTIONS

1. Reread the parable that Jesus gave us in Luke 18:1–8. Can you remember the dramatic contrasts between the unjust judge and our loving God?

2.   What are the five reasons why we should pray? Can you elaborate on each one as if you were trying to encourage someone else on the subject of prayer?

3.   What are the three hindrances to prayer? How can they be overcome?

4.   Is there a specific Psalm that you could find that you can use when you pray?

5.   Can you memorize the passage in Hebrews 4:14–16?

6.   Can you make a prayer journal using the Lord's Prayer (Matthew 6:9–13) as your outline? Can you set aside time for prayer each day using your journal as a guide?

7.   Can you keep a prayer journal to keep track of answered prayers?

QUESTIONS PEOPLE ASK

■ *If God is all-powerful, why does he need people to pray?*

Fellowship was broken in the Garden. God's first words to the first sinners were, *"Where are you?"* He never had to ask this question before. Of course, God knew where they were, but the question served to show us that sin brought immediate separation. Since that time God has chosen to use human beings to bridge the gap that exists because of the fall. God said to the people, *"You will be for me a kingdom of priests ..."* (Exodus 19:6). Prayer is an outworking of God's plan of redemption. We all hold the awesome responsibility to live up to our calling as priests.

Adam and Eve had stewardship over creation before the fall. Now those who have been redeemed have a new kind of stewardship after the cross. We exercise our stewardship as we fulfill our rightful place as priests before God. He will use us to bridge the gap that sin has created. God allows us to have a share in the responsibility of bringing his redemptive power to bear in our world.

Chapter Nine

WORSHIP

KEY POINTS

- The nature of true worship
- The nature of false worship
- Ways in which we can we express worship

Places of worship include temples, cathedrals, mosques, pagodas, synagogues, churches, basilicas, chapels, convents, monasteries, abbeys, pantheons, tabernacles, sanctuaries, shrines, and caves. Practices of worship can include a variety of rituals, incantations, prayers, songs, dances, ceremonies, liturgies, readings, celebrations, devotions, sacrifices, and bodily postures. The place of worship can be anywhere on earth where humanity exists. Most anthropologists will agree that anywhere you find human society you will also find some form of worship. There is the never-ending need for the transcendent.

What is it that links humanity with this one common thread? The answer is found in the fact that we were created for worship. God has built into us the capacity for worship, and it is an integral part of our makeup. Worship was the key issue before the fall, and it still is after the fall. In this chapter we will look at true worship and false worship. Then we will conclude with a discussion on expressions of worship.

Section One

TRUE WORSHIP

In the fourth chapter of John there is the remarkable account of Jesus and the woman at the well. She was given a personal guided tour into the true meaning of worship. Her tour guide was the Son of God. It doesn't get any better than this!

The woman was a complete outcast. She was an outcast culturally, politically, and morally. It was against cultural norms for a woman to have a conversation with a man, especially a rabbi, in broad daylight. In fact, the disciples were surprised that Jesus would breach such a social taboo (see John 4:27). Women were not on an equal social status with men in that culture. The woman was also a political outcast because she was a Samaritan. John made note of this with the comment, *"For Jews do not associate with Samaritans"* (John 4:9). You could say she also was a moral outcast, as Jesus pointed out by saying to her, *"The fact is, you have had five husbands, and the man you now have is not your husband"* (John 4:18).

Jesus intentionally sought her out. He not only made a deliberate trek through forbidden Samaritan territory, which undoubtedly made his disciples uncomfortable, but he asked the woman for a drink of water. This came as a great surprise to her. Could it have been that Jesus knew what he was doing? Yes, he was about to zero in on the central core of what constituted true worship. He chose to use a person representing the furthest from the ideal. He revealed the secrets of the kingdom of God to a person of the highest social standing (Nicodemus) in John 3. Now he addressed the essence of true worship to a person of the lowest social status in John 4. As their conversation progressed, it got deeper and deeper until Jesus introduced the essence of worship:

"Sir," the woman said, "I can see that you are a prophet. Our fathers worshiped on this mountain, but you Jews claim that the place where we must worship is in Jerusalem."

Jesus declared, "Believe me, woman, a time is coming when you will worship the Father neither on this mountain nor in Jerusalem. You Samaritans worship what you do not know; we worship what we do know, for salvation is from the Jews. Yet a time is coming and has now come when the true worshipers will worship the father in spirit and truth, for they are the kind of worshipers the Father seeks. God is spirit, and his worshipers must worship in spirit and in truth."

The woman said, "I know that Messiah (called Christ) is coming. When he comes, he will explain everything to us."

Then Jesus declared, "I who speak to you am he" (John 4:19–26).

Jesus broke open the secret of true worship. It was not a matter of location. It was not a matter of "this mountain" or "that city"—even if it was the city of Jerusalem itself. It was not a matter of any temple or shrine. It was not a matter of culture or politics. It was not a matter of gender or social status. Worship is a matter of spirit and of truth.

Spirit

"God is spirit, and his worshipers must worship him in spirit" (John 4:24). This was what Jesus explained to Nicodemus in the previous chapter of John.

"Flesh gives birth to flesh, but the Spirit gives birth to spirit. You should not be surprised at my saying, 'You must be born again.'" (John 3:6–7).

Consider Nicodemus in John, chapter three. Despite all of the human goodness exhibited in the life of Nicodemus, he was still a man born after the flesh. He was still a son of Adam. He was born with a fallen, sinful nature inherited from Adam. The sinful nature was conveyed in the word "flesh" that Jesus used. The unfortunate reality is that everyone born of Adam is born spiritually dead.

"When you eat of it you will surely die" (Genesis 2:17). Paul amplified this by reminding the Ephesian believers of the work that Jesus had done for them:

But because of his great love for us, God, who is rich in mercy, made us alive with Christ even when we were dead in transgressions (Ephesians 2:4–5).

The absolute necessity of being "born again" cannot be overstressed. To worship God in the spirit we must be born of the Holy Spirit. This happens as a supernatural act of God when a person receives Jesus Christ as Savior:

To all who received him, to those who believed in his name, he gave the right to become children of God—children born not of natural descent, nor of human decision or a husband's will, but born of God (John 1:12–13).

To be born again is to be given a new nature. The old nature being replaced by a new nature is foreshadowed in the Old Testament by the sign of the covenant. Our old sinful nature is, in effect, cut away, and the Holy Spirit gives us a new nature (spirit) through the new birth. The sign of the Old Covenant was circumcision. It was a prophetic act looking forward to its fulfillment in the work of Christ. It finds its ultimate fulfillment in the lives of believers living under the New Covenant.

Neither circumcision nor uncircumcision means anything; what counts is new creation (Galatians 6:15).

Circumcision is circumcision of the heart, by the Spirit (Romans 2:29).

If anyone is in Christ, he is a new creation; the old has gone, the new has come! (2 Corinthians 5:17).

It can be plainly seen in Scripture that the worship God is looking for is worship that is done in spirit. It is not a matter of geography, buildings, or of a person's nationality. It is a matter of new birth (new nature) brought about by the power of the Holy Spirit. Ultimately, it is about having a living relationship with God through Jesus Christ in the power of the Holy Spirit.

Truth

God must be worshiped for who he is and worshiped in the manner prescribed by him. True worship must be in accordance with God's nature and character. Anything less is not true worship. Notice that Jesus said to the woman at the well that God was seeking worshipers of a certain kind. God demands worship in spirit and in truth. This is not a secondary issue. True worship *is* the issue. An example comes from the famous account of the Ten Commandments:

And God spoke all these words: "I am the LORD your God, who brought you out of Egypt, out of the land of slavery. You shall have no other gods before me. You shall not make for yourself an idol in the form of anything in heaven above or on the earth below. You shall not bow down to them or worship them; for I, the LORD your God, am a jealous God . . ." (Exodus 20:1–5).

The whole issue before the children of Israel was whether or not they would accept God's offer. Would they worship him and only him? If the LORD would indeed be their God and they would be his people, then there were some stipulations that must be followed closely. The Ten Commandments were a summation of the stipulations that formed this covenant.

The first commandment pertained to exclusive worship: *"You shall have no other gods before me."* This was the first and greatest stipulation. It would eliminate all other gods. It would narrow the true definition of worship to be the exclusive province of the God of Abraham, Isaac, and Jacob. The gods of all the other nations would have to be eliminated.

This would lead to the next stipulation: the prohibition of idol worship. The nature of idol worship is that the worshiper crafts his/her own god and then bows down to it. If the first commandment was not kept, it would naturally lead to the breaking of the second commandment. Another god would take the place of the true God. It would be a god of the person's own making. It could be made by their hands to be seen with their eyes. It could also exist in the mind and remain unseen. People would not necessarily bow, but the god would exist nonetheless.

True worship demands that no idol, no image, no created thing can take God's rightful place as the one true God to be worshiped. When the apostle Paul traveled to Athens, he noticed that the people were very religious. There were temples to all sorts of gods. They even had a shrine dedicated to the unknown God just in case they had missed one. Paul used this as a means to communicate to them the truth of the one true God:

"Men of Athens! I see that in every way you are very religious. For as I walked around and looked carefully at your objects of worship, I even found an altar with this inscription: TO AN UNKNOWN GOD. Now what you worship as something unknown I am going to proclaim him to you" (Acts 17:22–23).

The people of Athens worshiped in ignorance. Paul gave them instructions about the true worship that the God of the universe required. Some believed, and some did not. This disparity still holds true today. Some will engage in true biblical worship, and others will refuse. This is nothing new. There will always be true worship coexisting with false worship. We need to be able to discern between the two.

Section Two

FALSE WORSHIP

<u>God determines True Worship</u>

A major lesson for all mankind is that God determines how we should worship. If he is worthy of worship, then it is reasonable to assume that his worshipers should be happy to follow his directions regarding worship. Sometimes this is a tough lesson to learn. Most human beings aren't too accepting of having someone else telling them what to do. We inherited this tendency from our first parents. Evidence of this weakness was found in the account of Cain and Abel.

Each of them brought an offering to God as an act of worship. Abel's offering was accepted, but Cain's offering was not. This made Cain very angry. The specific reason for God's rejection of Cain's offering was not given, but the end result proved that God knew what he was doing. It is instructive that God very graciously gave Cain the opportunity to make things right:

Then the LORD said to Cain, "Why are you angry? Why is your face downcast? If you do what is right, will you not be accepted? But if you do not do what is right, sin is crouching at your door; it desires to have you, but you must master it" (Genesis 4:6–7).

God gave Cain a second chance. He entreated him to do what was right. He also gave him a solemn warning. Cain responded by remaining angry and luring his brother into a trap that led to cold-blooded murder. Cain serves as a graphic lesson to all those who insist on remaining angry with God that he would dare to require a certain manner of worship. The lesson for us is that God sets the standards of worship, not us. He is the Creator; we are a part of his creation. The Bible speaks of this rejection of God's way as being *"the way of Cain"* (Jude 11). It is the way of the world that rejects Christ and God's prescribed standard of worship.

God is still saying to the world, *"Why are you so angry? Why is your face so downcast? If you do what is right, will you not be accepted?"* The right thing is to say, "Yes" to Jesus. Many people in this Christ-rejecting world still choose the way of Cain.

The Folly of Perverted Worship

Romans 1:18–32 contains a detailed account of false worship "gone to seed." Here it is in part:

The wrath of God is being revealed from heaven against all the godlessness and wickedness of men who suppress the truth by their wickedness, since what may be known about God is plain to them, because God has made it plain to them. For since the creation of the world God's invisible qualities–his eternal power and divine nature—have been clearly seen, being understood from what has been made, so that men are without excuse (Romans 1:18–20).

For although they know God, they neither glorified him as God nor gave thanks to him, but their thinking became futile and their foolish hearts were darkened. Although they claimed to be wise, they became fools and exchanged the glory of the immortal God for images made to look like mortal man and birds and animals and reptiles (Romans 1:21–23).

Furthermore, since they did not think it worthwhile to retain the knowledge of God, he gave them over to a depraved mind (Romans 1:28).

Notice in verse 18 that they *"suppress the truth by their wickedness."* It is a willful act. It is not a matter of intellect so much as it is a matter of the will. Such is *"the way of Cain."* The result is that a worship inversion takes place. Instead of the Creator being exalted, he is relegated to a lower position (v. 23) in exchange for things of this creation that are infinitely less than him. It is an exchange rate that is beyond calibration or calculation. There is no calibration for infinite loss. The only description that comes close is that the infinite glory of God is exchanged for mere copies of things that creep and crawl on this earth.

Worshiping in spirit and in truth is more than mere religion. It is more than a ritual. It requires new birth and a new way to relate to the God who made us. We live in a world of people who are ignorant of their need for a change in nature, and we live in a world full of people who hold to different gods. The challenge is to remain true to our God and at the same time live among the people of the world. We must live lives that glorify God, thus proving him to be worthy of worship.

Section Three

EXPRESSIONS OF WORSHIP

There are many ways that worship may be expressed. Worship can be a way of life. It can be expressed in the arts. It can be expressed through sacrificial living and through the giving of our resources. Worship can be expressed by singing praises and through prayer. Two broad aspects of worship are how we live and how we praise.

How We Live

When we think of worship, we should be aware that worship means much more than singing in church. Worship is meant to be a way of life. It is the very expression of the way we live and the choices we make in our daily lives. Paul compared this to offering our bodies as "living sacrifices." Because of all that God has done for us, our response should be to live for him like never before. We are to serve him in our daily lives. This is what Paul emphasized in the following passage:

Therefore, I urge you, brothers, in view of God's mercy, to offer your bodies as living sacrifices, holy and pleasing to God—this is your spiritual act of worship. Do not conform any longer to the pattern of this world, but be transformed by the renewing of your mind. Then you will be able to test and approve what God's will is—his good, pleasing and perfect will (Romans 12:1–2).

When Jesus was tempted by the devil, the issue of worship was specifically mentioned in one of the three temptations. The devil said that if Jesus would worship him, he would be given all the kingdoms of the world with all their glory and splendor.

Jesus answered, *"It is written: 'Worship the Lord your God and serve him only'"* (Luke 4:8).

The devil didn't say anything about *serving* him. Jesus rightly quoted from the Scriptures that worshiping God also means serving God. We serve whom we worship. As much as the devil would like us to overlook this little detail, service to God is the essence of worship. When Joshua challenged the people of Israel before they were to enter the Promised Land, he wanted to reaffirm that the issue of true worship be settled outright.

"Now fear the LORD and serve him with all faithfulness. Throw away the gods your forefathers worshiped beyond the River and in Egypt, and serve the LORD. But if serving the LORD seems undesirable to you, then choose for yourselves this day whom you will serve, whether the gods your forefathers served beyond the River, or the gods of the Amorites, in whose land you are living. But as for me and my household, we will serve the LORD" (Joshua 24:14–15).

Notice how worship and service were combined as one. This is the way of worship. There is no such thing as virtual Christianity. It is not something we do only for an hour on Sunday morning. We worship by the way we live and by the daily choices we make. Our entire lives are to be lived to glorify God every day. It has often been said that if Jesus is not Lord *of all*, he is not Lord *at all*.

TIME OUT

In the book of Romans, Paul took eleven chapters to lay out the gospel. It was not until *after* he had fully and carefully explained the miracle, grace, and power of the gospel that we were then given the exhortation on how to conduct our lives. The more we know the gospel, the more we will be empowered to live (worship) God. Go back and read the first eleven chapters of Romans to get a fresh view of all that we are given in Christ.

Now, write the Romans 12:1–2 passage on a piece of paper. Meditate and memorize this passage. Romans 12:1–2 is the key to true living worship:

"Therefore, I urge you, brothers, in view of God's mercy, to offer your bodies as living sacrifices, holy and pleasing to God—this is your spiritual act of worship. Do not conform any longer to the pattern of this world, but be transformed by the renewing of your mind. Then you will be able to test and approve what God's will is—his good, pleasing and perfect will" (Romans 12:1–2).

How We Praise

Worship is a way of life. It ascribes to God his worth and his rightful place in our lives. Worship is also expressed in praise and adoration through song. Hymns and songs help us to magnify God for who he is. Worship put to music is the fruit of a heart full of thanksgiving. We are to love the Lord with all of our heart, mind, soul, and strength. The use of music in worship helps to unify our whole being—our emotions, intellect, heart, and mind:

Shout for joy to the LORD, all the earth.
Worship the LORD with gladness; come before him with joyful songs.
Know that the LORD is God. It is he who made us, and we are his;
we are his people, the sheep of his pasture.

Enter his gates with thanksgiving and his courts with praise; give thanks to him and praise his name.
For the LORD is good and his love endures forever; his faithfulness continues through all generations (Psalm 100).

Praise the LORD. Praise God in his sanctuary; praise him in his mighty heavens.
Praise him for his acts of power; praise him for his surpassing greatness.
Praise him with the sounding of the trumpet, praise him with the harp and lyre,
Praise him with tambourine and dancing, praise him with the strings and flute.
Praise him with the clash of cymbals, praise him with the resounding cymbals.
Let everything that has breath praise the LORD. Praise the LORD (Psalm 150).

We were created to worship. When true worship finds its restoration through Christ, there should be an unleashing of heartfelt song giving praise to Jesus Christ, our Redeemer.

Worship Lessons from King David

If ever anyone in the Bible epitomized worship it was David. We know he was an accomplished musician, and many of the Psalms were attributed to him. King Saul would often call on David to sing and play the harp. David's worship soothed Saul's troubled mind. David and Saul were a study of contrasts. David had an affinity for worship, while Saul did not.

Passion

David was passionate about worship. During Saul's reign as king of Israel, the Ark of the Covenant was not in Jerusalem. It had been captured by the Philistines before Saul became king and later abandoned about ten miles outside Jerusalem in the city of Kiriath

Jearim. When Saul became king, he made no attempt to retrieve the Ark and to restore it to its rightful place as the center of worship for all of Israel. David, in stark contrast, made this one of his first acts when he became king. He made Jerusalem the capital and sought out the Ark to bring it into the holy city.

As the Ark was entering the city, David danced with joy, worshiping and praising God. Saul's daughter, Michal, who had become David's wife, witnessed this from her window. She despised him in her heart because she felt that such a public display of abandon was beneath the dignity of a king. David later rebuked her by saying it wasn't a public display for her, or anyone else's benefit, but it was unto the LORD. Furthermore, he said:

I will celebrate before the LORD. I will become even more undignified than this, and I will be humiliated in my own eyes (2 Samuel 6:21–22).

The first lesson we can learn from David is his passion for worship. This was a missing ingredient in Saul's life. David was passionate about worship, and it was his passion that made him *the* example of worship for us all. We do not have to dance with the abandon of King David, but we do need to invest our worship with like passion. This means that we need to block out competing thoughts and anything else that would serve as a distraction from true, heartfelt worship. We don't want to find ourselves going to church, singing a bunch of songs, and then going home as if nothing of consequence had taken place. We might even need to proclaim to our own hearts, just as David did to Michal, *"I will celebrate before the Lord!"* It may require a pronouncement centered upon the will to worship. Passion often begins with our will.

In the game of football, if the offensive team fails to move the ball in their first three allotted chances, their fourth and last chance usually means that they will have to punt the ball away to the other team. This is expressed in the phrase "three-and-out." It has become a figure of speech for a lackluster performance. One might be asked how their team did in their last series, and the answer would come back, "Oh, they went 'three-and-out.'" We don't want to have "three-and-out" worship. We don't want to have lackluster worship due to a lack of passion.

There is plenty to get passionate about as a believer. There may or may not be any outward sign of passion to be seen by people. What is essential is that our will and our minds be fully engaged. We must focus all of our heart and minds on the One worthy of worship. We must fight off distractions and self-centeredness and give to God what is due him. You could even say that this is what makes up the "discipline" of worship.

Encouragement

There is another lesson we can learn from the life of David: he knew how to encourage himself in the Lord. There was an incident when David and his followers set up camp at Ziklag. The women and children were left behind while David and his army were out engaged in warfare. When they returned, they found that the Amalekites raided the camp, and everything was destroyed. The women and children were nowhere to be found. The Bible says that David and all his men saw this and wept aloud until they had no more strength left to weep.

The next thing we read is that the men were angry and talked of killing David. There could hardly be a worse situation for David. This was a time when he was running for his life from King Saul. On top of losing his whole family to the Amalekites, he now had his own army against him, too.

This account is compressed in six little verses in 1 Samuel 30:1–6. There is a short phrase tacked on at the end of verse six that could be passed over very easily if it is not read carefully. *"But David found strength in the LORD his God."* Then, suddenly in verse seven, we read where David began to organize his men with a miraculous sense of confidence. They rallied together, pursued the Amalekites, and rescued every single family member. All was recovered.

How did David do this? Of course the LORD was with him in his pursuit, but how did he recover from such overwhelming odds and under what must have been crushing emotional agony? The answer is somewhere in the mystery that lies between verse six and verse seven. We aren't told, but we are given a clue. *"David found strength in the LORD his God."* It is very possible that somehow in the midst of all the anger and suffering of the men, David got off by himself and had some kind of worship/prayer session with the LORD.

Undoubtedly he had done this before. All we need do is read some of his Psalms. The Psalms were often sung. Perhaps David reached back in his memory of all that God had done through him in the past. *"The LORD is my Shepherd . . . He restores my soul . . . Even though I walk through the valley of the shadow of death, I will fear no evil for you are with me"* (Psalm 23). *"O LORD, how many are my foes! How many rise up against me. Many are saying of me, 'God will not deliver him.' But you are a shield around me, O LORD; you bestow glory on me and lift up my head"* (Psalm 3:1–3). We could go on, but the point is that worship is rich in strength and encouragement. Furthermore, we know that, for David, it led to victory.

David was not the only one who received the benefit of the encouragement he received. It spread throughout the camp. The same will be true in our own lives as well. Worship is a powerful means of eliciting the help of God and bringing encouragement to the whole body of Christ through those who will give themselves to worship.

CONCLUSION

It is important to stress that the foundation of our worship must be centered on the worthiness of God. We worship God because God is worthy. Whenever we find ourselves struggling to get into an attitude of worship, it will help us if we will forget all other things and just focus on the worthiness of God. Worship starts with God. In fact, the very dictionary definition for the word "worship" is "Worth-ship" or, ascribing worth. Let us praise God, for he is indeed worthy.

APPLAUSE ALERT

Sometimes people who are new to worship can be intimidated by the false idea that there is some kind of performance expectation when it comes to singing to the Lord. This can be the natural carryover from a lifetime of watching and enjoying very talented people in the various performing arts. Worship is completely different. While there are certainly people who are gifted and have amazing musical abilities, every believer is invited to give himself or herself to worship, regardless of musical ability.

"Worship the LORD with gladness; come before him with joyful songs" (Psalm 100:2). If we wait until we are perfect singers, we may never get started. We are not worshiping for the applause of people, but for the glory of God. Give it all you've got next time. This is an ALERT to help us remember that *God* is the center of worship. The center of worship will always be the One who is the center of the universe and of our lives. Worship God.

STUDY QUESTIONS

1. Read John 4:4–26. How would you explain to someone that true worship is not dependent on geographic location, gender, social status or nationality?

2. What kind of worshipers did Jesus say God was looking for?

3. Can you define what it means to worship God in spirit?

4. Can you define what it means to worship God in truth?

5. Read Romans 1:18–32. How many ways is false worship described and what are some of the repercussions?

6.   What did Jesus say in answer to Satan's temptation that proves that a major part of worship is in how we choose to live?

7.   What two lessons can we learn about worship from the life of King David?

QUESTIONS PEOPLE ASK

■ *Why would God make such a big deal about worship being exclusively to him?*

This can be answered from two points of view: first from God's point of view, and then from the point of view of those who worship him.

Who God is — What God has done

It was no accident that God began the stipulations of the Covenant with the first commandment that he, and only he, be worshiped. We can learn the reason why this was so by considering the preamble to the Ten Commandments. *"I am the LORD your God, who brought you out of Egypt, out of the land of slavery"* (Exodus 20:2). The people were in cruel and bitter slavery for 400 years. The United States has been in existence for a little over 200 years and yet it might seem to us like it has been forever. How much more would 400 years seem like forever? That's the whole point. It was an impossible situation.

This is the issue as seen from the side of God. Who else could have performed such a miraculous feat in such a miraculous manner with such miraculous results? The answer is "No one!" The issue of exclusive worship is that God alone is worthy. No one else is like him. No other so-called god could have done what he has done. The people who are in covenant with him owe their absolute allegiance to him, not to mention their gratitude.

To demand exclusive worship is a natural result of who God is *and* what he has done for the people who are called by his name. Imagine the outrageous insult, for the people so graciously and miraculously rescued and loved, to give their worship to another. It would be a slap in the face. It would be an inexcusable insult. It would be crazy. Therefore, the demand for exclusive worship makes perfect sense in view of all that God has done and for the reality of his true nature and identity.

God Is the One True God

From the point of view of the people, the demand for exclusive worship can be seen as motivated by God's love. God loves his people to the utmost. Who else can provide better for them than the Creator of the universe? He has proved himself again and again. The folly of the people giving their worship to another god is that these other gods can do nothing. The other nations may have their so-called gods, but they are not gods at all:

Why do the nations say, "Where is their God?" Our God is in heaven; he does whatever pleases him. But their idols are silver and gold, made by the hands of men. They have mouths, but cannot speak, eyes but they cannot see; they have ears, but cannot hear, noses, but they cannot smell; they have hands, but cannot feel, feet, but they cannot walk; nor can they utter a sound with their throats. Those who make them will be like them, and so will all who trust in them (Psalm 115:2–8).

These so-called gods are nothing. All who follow them can receive no help from them. This is where the danger begins. False teaching will eventually follow as well. The ultimate danger in worshiping other gods is that it will keep the worshiper from a right relationship with the true living God. Paul made the point that, in reality, these are not gods. He related this fact to those who may have had a problem eating food that had been sacrificed to idols (gods):

We know that an idol in nothing at all in the world and that there is no God but one. For even if there are so-called gods, whether in heaven or on earth (as indeed there are many "gods" and many "lords"), yet for us there is but one God, the Father, from whom all things came and for whom we live; and there is but one Lord, Jesus Christ, though whom all things came and through whom we live. But not everyone knows this (1 Corinthians 8:4–7).

Furthermore, the gods offer no gospel. The gospel is good news. These gods can only offer bad news. They have a "bad-spel"—bad news. What they do offer will not bring salvation, as Paul teaches in his letter to the Galatians:

I am astonished that you are so quickly deserting the one who called you by the grace of Christ and are turning to a different gospel—which is really no gospel at all (Galatians 1:6–7).

The issue of exclusive worship is an essential doctrine. There is only one God who saves. There is only one gospel. Human worship to another god robs God of his glory and condemns the false worshiper for all eternity. It is because of God's love that he desires to save all people from the travesty of false worship.

■ *I don't bow down to idols. So how can I be an idol worshiper?*

Remember, an idol is any idea or thing that takes the place of the One True God. Whatever takes the place of God is an idol. Many idols are invisible because we worship them in our minds. We may not be involved in declared and gross idol worship. However, if we have things in our lives that have usurped God's place, then we might have an idol. Think of an idol as an altar. Is there an altar to which you bring the sacrifices of your time, talent and treasure? Such an altar may identify an idol that has been given worth (worthiness) greater than God.

Thank God that through Jesus Christ we are no longer idolaters. However, we can always be tempted, and we may make mistakes.

When we sense that we might be out of balance, it is time to repent. The Holy Spirit will use these times to cleanse us and draw us closer to the Lord.

It could be possible that the last idol to go for most people is that ever-present idol: self. We may find ourselves to be our own gods. We want to rule and to reign over our own lives. When we truly bow and repent, then God will take up his rightful place on the throne of our lives.

Chapter Ten

REVIEW

W hy a chapter for review? Review means to take another look. That's what we'll be doing. However, we will be taking another look with a goal in mind. The goal is to not only know the material a little better, but to know it well enough so that you will be able to help someone else grow in their Christian faith. This is one of the keys to discipleship. This is the heart of the ministry of *Christian Basics*. Paul said to Timothy:

The things you have heard me say in the presence of many witnesses entrust to reliable men who will also be qualified to teach others (2 Timothy 2:2).

We will review a little bit from each of the last nine chapters in *Christian Basics*. In each review there will be challenges to see the various topics in new ways. Along with these challenges is the goal of becoming someone that God can use in the life of another. To help someone else in the faith is a major goal of discipleship.

■ Chapter One—The Truth Shall Set You Free

It is important as we work through biblical truth to be able to understand what it means to believe. Jesus said that truth exists and that we can know the truth. Knowledge of truth and belief work together. We are called believers. We believe in Jesus Christ, and we believe in his teachings as being truthful. It is important to test truth because ideas have consequences that go far beyond mere words. What starts as an idea may soon develop into an ideology. An ideology can then become a way of life. It doesn't take much to notice that not all ways of life lead to a life that would please Jesus.

In the first chapter, the "The Two L Test" was introduced. We can apply this test to any idea or philosophy of life by asking two questions: is it Logical and Livable? First, does the idea make sense? Second, can we live out the idea in the real world?

For example, some say, "All roads lead to God." Does this make sense? If we applied the same logic, then we could also say that all roads lead to the place where you live? That statement makes no sense. The statement flunks the test of the first L—logic.

Let's try the second L. Is the statement livable? Can we apply the logic of "All roads lead to the place where you live" in the real world? Imagine if you were a few hundred miles from your hometown. You open a map book to find the way to your town. You are surprised to see that the map book contains only one page with only *one* road. You look hard for an explanation and you are told, "All roads lead to the place where you live." Not only does it not make sense (not logical), but you could not live it (not livable). Truth must conform to reality.

The main goal of chapter one -- The Truth Shall Set You Free -- is to develop an understanding of our worldview. We should be able to explain what we believe and why we believe. Our worldview should be both logical and livable. As we develop a clear understanding of our worldview, the Bible and the gospel will become God's shepherd's staff to help us in this crazy, mixed-up world. We will be more able to help others come to a living faith in the one who said, *"I Am the truth."*

Below is a list of books geared to helping people develop a biblical worldview. This is a partial list of suggested books and authors. You may develop your own favorites, but here are a few:

I Don't have Enough Faith to Be an Atheist by Norman Geisler and Frank Turek

Mere Christianity by C. S. Lewis

A Shattered Visage, the Real Face of Atheism by Ravi Zacharias

Life's Ultimate Questions by Ronald Nash

■ Chapter Two—The Bible

When you hold a Bible in your hand, you are holding a miracle. Do miracles happen? If you are reading a Bible, you are participating in a miracle. You can have a miracle in your life every day. We have a book that has stood the test of time and experience for thousands of years. This fact speaks well of God's providence. He has provided a useful tool for his people to learn about him.

Psalm 119 is a hymn to the power and majesty of the Word of God. Read this psalm and let the majesty and mystery of God's Word sink into your heart. You will find that God's Word is called by many names: laws, statutes, precepts, decrees, commands, and God's Word. One of the prayers in verse 18 asks of God, *"Open my eyes that I may see wonderful things in your law."* This is a prayer God will answer.

Just as God saw to it that his people had manna in the wilderness, he will see to it that we have the manna of his Word in our wilderness journey on this earth. The children of Israel had to make the effort to retrieve the manna for themselves. Receiving God's manna required effort. Learning the Word of God will take time and effort as well. God will not do the reading for us, but he has promised to enlighten us through his Word. Our reward will be well-fed hearts and minds. We then will be strengthened and enabled to be used to help others.

Below is a partial list of books and that may be of help. Add your own favorites to this list as you study and grow in your faith and in your ability to be used of God in the lives of others.

A General Introduction to the Bible by Norman Geisler and William Nix

The Canon of Scripture by F.F. Bruce

How to Read the Bible for All Its Worth by Gordon Fee and Douglas Stewart

Introduction to Biblical Interpretation by William Klein, Craig Blomberg and Robert Hubbard

Scripture Twisting, by James Sire

Playing by the Rules, by Robert Stein

■ Chapter Three—Jesus

The identity of Jesus is a crucial part of Christianity. Without Jesus we have no Christianity. If Jesus is not who he said he was and who the Bible declares him to be, we have no basis for our faith. This is why it is of utmost importance that we study Jesus.

Time as we know it will end when Jesus returns. All of humanity will then know who Jesus is. For many it will be too late. This is the sad reality of this life. This is also the reason why learning and growing in the faith is so important. We must get to the point where we can go confidently out into God's harvest field.

Here are a few books that will help in obtaining a better biblical view of the nature of Jesus Christ. As you pursue your love for Jesus Christ, you will develop your own library. Try one of these books as you move forward in your faith. As you gradually build your faith stronghold, God will use you to help others.

The Case for Christ by Lee Strobel

Christ Among Other gods by Erwin Lutzer

Jesus Under Fire by Michael Wilkins and J. P. Moreland

■ Chapter Four—Salvation

SOS is a well-known distress signal for life-threatening situations. Our world needs to send out an SOS. Our problem is there is no person in this world that can help us. We are all lost. This is where the gospel comes in. The gospel is *the* answer sent from beyond this realm. The gospel is the only remedy in the universe. The gospel is the only answer known to humanity that can look the problem of sin and death square in the face and provide the remedy. The gospel not only tells the gospel-truth about our predicament, but also provides the cure. There is no other gospel than the good news of Jesus Christ.

Every believer should learn ways of presenting the saving message of salvation to others. There are many resources available to help people learn any number of techniques and skills for presenting the gospel.

There are many organizations that specialize in sharing the gospel, such as:

■ www.livingwaters.com
■ www.cru.org

Your own church or denomination may have materials for evangelism that you might be available for you. The objective is to be able to share your faith in an effective way.

■ Chapter Five—The Church

Have you ever had someone knock at your door and tell you that you must belong to their church? They could be a Jehovah's Witness or a Mormon elder, but their thinking about what it means to belong to a church is the same. You must belong to *their* organization (church) or you are in error. The true error lies in having a concept of the church as something we join and, by following some set of rules, or meeting certain criteria, we now belong. This is not the concept of church in the orthodox Christian understanding. In the true Christian and biblical sense, if you are born again, then you *are* the church.

That being understood, there are many denominations (names) of churches that are legitimate. God allows for freedom in many secondary issues. A study of the many different denominations that exist will help give you a broader base from which to understand your own church fellowship. The more we understand how church fellowships are organized today, the better we will be able to have a healthy and mature view of what a church fellowship is supposed to be. There are many church organizations that differ due to doctrines and worship preferences. However, if they hold to the essentials of the Christian faith, they are legitimate in the eyes of the Lord. We will see people of other church fellowships as brothers and sisters in the Lord. That is a good thing.

One way to develop a healthy view of what makes a church is to study church history. A good book to get started is *Church History in Plain Language* by Bruce Shelley.

■ Chapter Six—The Trinity

The Trinity is a mystery. Many people like mystery novels, but in the end, they like the mystery solved. God is totally beyond our comprehension. However, he has revealed himself to us in a beautiful way in our Holy Scripture. He has revealed himself as three-in-one.

Perhaps it would be good to study the history of the doctrine and to dig a little deeper into the mystery of the Trinity of God. There are a number of good books that can be of great help. Any reliable and trustworthy book on the doctrines of the Christian faith would be helpful. You may slowly build your own library and become more and more comfortable embracing the majesty and the mystery of the nature of the God whom we serve. Below are two books that are helpful:

The Forgotten Trinity by James White

God in Three Persons by Calvin Beisner

■ Chapter Seven—Discipleship

When people enter into a discipleship relationship with the Lord, they are entering into God's ultimate plan for all believers. You may recall the famous last words of Jesus in Matthew 28 that we are to go into all the world and make disciples of all people. Maybe you've also heard the saying, "Disciples are not born; they are made." The book you hold in your hand, *Christian Basics,* was written to help fulfill the mandate set by Jesus. There are many other books and resources that will help as well.

You have read this far because you are willing to learn. Your attitude of humble submission before the Lord prepares your discipleship to become fruitful. Your fruitfulness is energized by your daily affirmation to the Lord, "Not my will, but yours."

The first place to learn how to obey the will of God may be in your family: husbands, wives, fathers, mothers, and sons and daughters. The circle expands to your school or workplace. The ever-widening circle extends to the marketplace and our secular social interactions. In short, we learn how to obey in all we do. Your local church is an opportunity to live out God's will in grateful obedience. There are many ways to serve and learn to serve in our local churches.

There are many good books available to aid us in developing a life of discipleship as we follow the Lord. Here are a few:

The Lost Art of Disciple Making by Leroy Eims

Spiritual Leadership by Oswald Chambers

*Discipleship by G. Campbell Morga*n

■ Chapter Eight—Prayer

The best way to grow in prayer is to begin praying. We learn by doing. Also, we will find that the more we pray, the more we will find prayer to be a blessed calling. We will have a prayer diary, a prayer list, a prayer time, and a prayer life. Prayer is our way of fulfilling God's call in our lives of being priests before him. In prayer, we present all of our needs and the needs of others before the Sovereign Lord of the universe.

Prayer is a way of bringing encouragement to those around us. "I have you in my prayers." Or, "How may I pray for you?" No one may even know about whom or for what you are praying. Your faith will be built up, and you will be fulfilling your duty and love as one who belongs to the Lord. You will notice if you go to a prayer meeting, with like-minded people, you will never go away discouraged. Prayer brings encouragement.

There are many devotional books on prayer that will serve to encourage you in developing a rich prayer life.

With Christ in the School of Prayer by Andrew Murray

Any book on prayer by E. M. Bounds

Praying the Scriptures by Judson Cornwall

■ Chapter Nine—Worship

One way to develop worship is to realize that how we live is worship. The decisions we make and the attitudes we hold in our hearts are all part of how we worship. *"You shall have no other gods before me"* (Exodus 20:3) is at the heart of worship. You can keep your decisions and your attitudes between you and God. No one needs to know how you are yielding your life more and more to God's will.

A powerful source of expressing worship is music. You can begin to collect worship recordings that move your heart to the Lord. Another challenge is to pick up a musical instrument and begin learning the art of music along with worship. You may be surprised that as the years go by you will be used to help and encourage others to worship in song.

My prayers are with you as you use this book to strengthen your faith. I pray that God will bless you and use you mightily in his service. Here is a prayer for you as you begin to move out in service to the Lord.

The LORD bless you and keep you;
The LORD make his face shine upon you and be gracious to you;
The LORD turn his face toward you and give you peace.
Numbers 6:24–26

CPSIA information can be obtained at www.ICGtesting.com
Printed in the USA
BVOW09s0619290914

368601BV00005B/12/P